Oxford Uni~ Press   ~/~   =5.00

D0252824

DISCARD

# CUSTODIAL RIGHTS

*by*
Margaret C. Jasper

Oceana's Legal Almanac Series:
*Law for the Layperson*

# Oceana Publications

You may order this or any Oceana publication by visiting Oceana's
website at http://www.oceanalaw.com

Library of Congress Control Number: 2006922578

ISBN 0-19-532153-7
ISBN 978-0-19-532153-1

Oceana's Legal Almanac Series: Law for the Layperson
ISSN 1075-7376

©2006 Oxford University Press, Inc.

To My Husband Chris

Your love and support
are my motivation and inspiration

-and-

In memory of my son, Jimmy

# Table of Contents

## CHAPTER 3:
## VISITATION

## CHAPTER 4:
## CUSTODIAL INTERFERENCE

**CHAPTER 5:**
**CHILD SUPPORT**

**CHAPTER 6:**
**CHILD ABUSE AND NEGLECT**

**CHAPTER 7:**
**ESTABLISHING PATERNITY**

## CHAPTER 8:
## REPRODUCTIVE TECHNOLOGY AND CUSTODY

## APPENDICES

# ABOUT THE AUTHOR

MARGARET C. JASPER is an attorney engaged in the general practice of law in South Salem, New York, concentrating in the areas of personal injury and entertainment law. Ms. Jasper holds a Juris Doctor degree from Pace University School of Law, White Plains, New York, is a member of the New York and Connecticut bars, and is certified to practice before the United States District Courts for the Southern and Eastern Districts of New York, the United States Court of Appeals for the Second Circuit, and the United States Supreme Court.

Ms. Jasper has been appointed to the law guardian panel for the Family Court of the State of New York, is a member of a number of professional organizations and associations, and is a New York State licensed real estate broker operating as Jasper Real Estate, in South Salem, New York.

In 2004, Ms. Jasper successfully argued a case before the New York Court of Appeals which gives mothers of babies who are stillborn due to medical negligence the right to bring a legal action and recover emotional distress damages. This successful appeal overturned a 26-year old New York case precedent, which previously prevented mothers of stillborn babies from suing their negligent medical providers.

Margaret Jasper maintains a website at http://www.JasperLawOffice. com.

Ms. Jasper is the author and general editor of the following legal almanacs:

AIDS Law
The Americans with Disabilities Act
Animal Rights Law
The Law of Attachment and Garnishment
Auto Leasing
Bankruptcy Law for the Individual Debtor

Individual Bankruptcy and Restructuring
Banks and their Customers
Becoming a Citizen
Buying and Selling Your Home
The Law of Buying and Selling
The Law of Capital Punishment
The Law of Child Custody
Your Rights in a Class Action Suit
Commercial Law
Consumer Rights Law
The Law of Contracts
Co-ops and Condominiums: Your Rights and Obligations As Owner
Copyright Law
Credit Cards and the Law
The Law of Debt Collection
Dictionary of Selected Legal Terms
The Law of Dispute Resolution
Drunk Driving Law
DWI, DUI and the Law
Education Law
Elder Law
Employee Rights in the Workplace
Employment Discrimination Under Title VII
Environmental Law
Estate Planning
Everyday Legal Forms
Executors and Personal Representatives: Rights and Responsibilities
Harassment in the Workplace
Health Care and Your Rights
Hiring Household Help and Contractors: Your Rights and Obligations Under the Law
Home Mortgage Law Primer
Hospital Liability Law
How To Change Your Name
How To Protect Your Challenged Child
Identity Theft and How To Protect Yourself
Injured on the Job: Employee rights, Worker's Compensation and Disability
Insurance Law
The Law of Immigration
International Adoption
Juvenile Justice and Children's Law
Labor Law

Landlord-Tenant Law
Lemon Laws
The Law of Libel and Slander
Living Together: Practical Legal Issues
Marriage and Divorce
The Law of Medical Malpractice
Motor Vehicle Law
The Law of No-Fault Insurance
Nursing Home Negligence
The Law of Obscenity and Pornography
Patent Law
The Law of Personal Injury
The Law of Premises Liability
Prescription Drugs
Privacy and the Internet: Your Rights and Expectations Under the Law
Probate Law
The Law of Product Liability
Real Estate Law for the Homeowner and Broker
Religion and the Law
Retirement Planning
The Right to Die
Rights of Single Parents
Law for the Small Business Owner
Small Claims Court
Social Security Law
Special Education Law
The Law of Speech and the First Amendment
Teenagers and Substance Abuse
Trademark Law
Victim's Rights Law
The Law of Violence Against Women
Welfare: Your Rights and the Law
Your Rights Under the Family and Medical Leave Act
You've Been Fired: Your Rights and Remedies
What if it Happened to You: Violent Crimes and Victims' Rights
What if the Product Doesn't Work: Warranties & Guarantees
Workers' Compensation Law
and Your Child's Legal Rights: An Overview.

# INTRODUCTION

One of the most difficult and painful tasks judges are asked to undertake is to determine a child custody award. The judge, a virtual stranger to the broken family, is asked to decide what is best for the innocent child when his or her mother and father wish to part. The child's psychological health tends to be overlooked by both parties.

Determining child custody is a task which most courts would rather be worked out amicably by the two adults who have created the situation. Unfortunately, given the fact that these cases are generally bitterly fought and filled with emotion, the court, as an impartial arbiter of the facts, must involve itself to protect the child.

This almanac explores the law of child custody, and provides a brief history of child custody decision-making in the United States. The modern-day standards by which courts award custody is discussed, including the factors a court considers in making a custody determination. The various types of custody arrangements presently available are also examined.

The custodial rights of unmarried parents and stepparents is also discussed, as well as recent rulings concerning the parental status of same-sex partners. The impact of reproductive technology in custody cases is also examined. The almanac also explores interstate and international custody litigation, and parental child abduction, as well as the custody-related topics of visitation, paternity, child support, and child abuse.

The Appendix provides applicable statutes, resource directories, and other pertinent information and data. The Glossary contains definitions of many of the terms used throughout the almanac.

# CHAPTER 1:
# HISTORICAL BACKGROUND

## THE ENGLISH COMMON LAW AND COLONIAL AMERICA

Under early English common law, children were viewed primarily as a cheap source of labor. They were often sent away from their families at a very early age and placed into apprenticeship. If they resisted, they were subject to punishment, such as imprisonment or banishment. At that time, custody of the children was awarded solely to the fathers.

Many children emigrated to the colonies as part of a forced labor market, some without parents to accompany them to the New World. Treatment of children in colonial America followed the harsh English tradition. At a very young age, usually at about 10 years old, children were placed into apprenticeship or sent off to serve another family in indentured servitude.

The custody of children was largely dependent on the economic needs of the colonies. A child born out-of-wedlock, once weaned, was often taken from the mother and placed with a "master." Under common-law, neither the father nor the mother was legally entitled to custody of an illegitimate child. Slave children were subject to sale at any age.

Women had few rights under colonial law. Divorce was rare. However, if it did occur, the father had an absolute right to custody unless he was proven unfit. The underlying assumption was that fathers would be better able to financially support their children, as well as provide for their training and education in order to make them productive members of society.

If the father died, custody rights were often assigned, either by will or court order, to a male guardian. In the rare instance a mother was able to gain custody, the father was no longer obligated to financially support his children.

## THE EMERGENCE OF THE TENDER YEARS DOCTRINE

In the mid to late nineteenth century, the law was expanded to permit mothers to retain custody of children under the age of seven—the so-called "Tender Years Doctrine." It provided for a maternal preference with respect to the custody of young children, unless the mother was proven unfit.

In a drastic turnabout, the "Tender Years Doctrine" was adopted in virtually every jurisdiction, and mothers were given custody in almost all contested custody cases. This maternal preference continued to prevail in custody decisions until the mid-1980s, when a trend toward equal custody rights emerged.

## THE "BEST INTERESTS OF THE CHILD" STANDARD

Beginning with the feminist movement of the 1960's, through the next several decades, virtually all jurisdictions eliminated the maternal preference by case law or statute. The new standard to be relied on was a custody determination that was in the "best interests of the child." Theoretically, fathers—including unwed fathers—were given an equal right to obtain custody.

Although there have been rapid advances towards fair and equal determinations of custody between fathers and mothers, it should be noted that many judges still retain the notion that mothers are better caretakers of young children. This attitude is often reflected in their custody decisions. However, if challenged, a judge's decision to give preference to a parent on the basis of sex would most likely be held unconstitutional. The "best interests of the child" standard is still the rule by which the courts are supposed to award custody.

## ADVENT OF THE JOINT CUSTODY ARRANGEMENT

Although the child's best interests are still paramount in custody decisions today, the trend has been to award joint custody to parents following divorce. It was recognized that awarding sole custody to one parent, and limited visitation to the non-custodial parent, undermined the non-custodial parent's relationship with his or her child, and created an atmosphere of "alienation." The child development experts acknowledged the importance of both the mother and father's contributions to a child's development, and continued parental involvement by both parents was beneficial.

Important societal changes during this time period also supported the joint custody arrangement. Fathers began to take a more "hands on" role in child rearing as the "two-income" household became the norm.

As a result, the first joint custody statute was enacted in California in 1979. By 1991, more than 40 states enacted statutes that allowed for a joint custody arrangement as either an option or preference, and the case law of most of the remaining states followed this trend.

Joint custody is discussed more fully in Chapter 2 of this almanac.

# CHAPTER 2:
# DETERMINING CUSTODY

## WHO IS A PARENT?

### Biological Parent

Most custody cases involve the rights of the child's biological parents. A biological parent—also referred to as a "natural parent"—refers to the man whose sperm, or woman whose egg, was used to produce the child. In most cases, the biological parents have the legal right to seek custody of, or visitation with, their biological child, unless their parental rights have been terminated or they voluntarily gave the child up for adoption. In addition, a man serving merely as a sperm donor, although the biological parent, would not be considered the legal parent and has no custody or visitation rights.

However, case law continues to evolve and grant ever-expanding custodial and visitation rights to other adults who have had a significant relationship with the child who is the subject of custody litigation. Following are the various names and roles that have been used to describe these non-biological parents.

### Adoptive Parent

An adoptive parent is an adult who has legally adopted a child after the biological parents' rights were terminated. The biological parents no longer have any custody or visitation rights once a legal adoption has taken place. Those rights, as well as the obligation to support the child, are transferred to the adoptive parent. If adoptive parents divorce, they both have the right to seek custody of, or visitation with, the adoptive child assuming both parents legally adopted the child.

### Stepparent

A stepparent is an adult who married a child's mother or father. In general, a stepparent does not have any custody rights or support obligation if he or she divorces the child's legal parent, unless the stepparent adopted the child. Nevertheless, in many states, a stepparent may petition the court for custody and/or visitation rights if he or she claims to be the child's "psychological" or "equitable" parent, as discussed below.

### Psychological Parent

A psychological parent is an adult who has established a strong and significant emotional attachment with a child, although the psychological parent is not legally responsible for the child. A psychological parent may argue that severing his or her relationship with the child would be detrimental to the health and well-being of the child.

### Equitable Parent

An equitable parent is similar to a psychological parent in that the adult has formed a strong emotional bond with a non-biological child such that they are considered to have a parent/child relationship and/or the biological parent has encouraged this type of relationship. The custody and visitation rights of an "equitable" parent arose to deal with situations where a husband has been led to believe he was the biological parent of the child but subsequently finds out through paternity testing that he is not the child's father.

A stepparent could also claim equitable parenthood when seeking custody or visitation of his or her stepchild when the biological parent is deceased. If a court grants custody or visitation to an equitable parent, that parent will also be required to contribute to the support of the child.

## THE IMPACT OF DIVORCE

When a childless marriage fails, the parties to the divorce are able to walk away from the relationship and move on with their lives. This is not possible in a divorce involving children. While divorce may end the role of spouse, it does not end the role of parent.

The impact of divorce on a child can be devastating. Divorce often results in drastic changes in the child's lifestyle. He or she must adjust to a radically different relationship with either parent. Instead of coming home to a two-parent family, time is now "scheduled" with the non-custodial parent. Family life as the child knew it is never the same.

No longer married, the parents must, for the sake of the child, maintain a certain level of amicable communication. Much of the trauma associated with divorce can be lessened, or possibly eliminated, if the parents work together to try and maintain as "normal" a life for the child as possible under the circumstances. The emotional well-being of the child following a divorce should be of paramount concern to both parents. For example, every effort must be made to resolve custody and visitation issues without involving the child.

Unfortunately, this is not always the case. Children are often used in harmful ways by one or both of the parents engaged in an adversarial divorce. For example, the child may be viewed as a convenient "bargaining chip" in divorce negotiations, particularly where financial issues are concerned. Children are often used as "spies" who must report back to the other side on what goes on in each other's households.

Bitterness between ex-spouses may lead to programming the child with negative, misleading and erroneous information about the other spouse. A common problem involves "brainwashing" of the child by one parent against the other. This destructive behavior can have devastating long-term effects on the child. A brainwashed child may accept all of the negative programming and purposely alienate themselves from the other parent. Thus, they lose out on what would likely be a very significant factor in their overall development. They deprive themselves of a loving parent and, as a consequence, they are also deprived of the extended family attached to that parent.

A brainwashed child seeks to gain favor in the sight of the offending parent by joining in the denigration of the other parent. Unfortunately, this behavior is usually encouraged and rewarded by the offending parent. The child, however, may harbor inner feelings of guilt and anxiety. Whether purposeful or unconscious, this type of behavior must be stopped to avoid irreparable psychological harm. If necessary, a change of physical custody and therapeutic intervention to "de-program" the child may be the only solution.

Whatever differences the adults may have with each other, this kind of activity confuses and further burdens the child who is already devastated by the breakup of their family unit. The best interests of the child should always be in the forefront to prevent irreparable psychological damage that will stay with the child on into adulthood, and carry over into his or her own parenting behavior.

In general, development of a "positive" post-divorce situation includes the involvement of—and cooperation between—both parents in the day-to-day lives of the child. This includes the absence of parental conflict, maintenance of stability and consistency in both households, and the involvement of the extended family.

### FACTORS TO BE CONSIDERED

Although the rules vary from state to state, most courts determining child custody take into account certain factors and generally award custody according to the standard known as "the best interests of the child."

### Best Interests of the Child

There are a number of factors which a Court considers in reaching a custody decision, including:

1. the emotional ties between the parent and child;

2. the mental and physical health of the parent;

3. the parent's ability to provide a stable and nurturing environment for the child;

4. the parental preference of a child who is of sufficient age and maturity;

5. the willingness of the proposed custodial parent to cooperate in encouraging a good relationship between the child and the non-custodial parent.

6. the age of the child;

7. the gender of the child;

8. the mental and physical health of the child;

9. any history of child neglect or abuse;

10. the ability of the parent to provide the child with necessities, e.g., food, shelter, clothing and health care;

11. any routine or living pattern already established for the child concerning school, home, community, etc.; and

12. the child's preference, if the child is above a certain age.

In addition, the court may order a home study and/or psychological evaluations of the parties and the child, before making a custody determination.

In many jurisdictions, the court may appoint a law guardian who makes an impartial determination as to which parent would make the better custodian of the child. The law guardian, whose role is to serve as the lawyer for the child, takes into account the child's wishes in making this determination, also considering the child's age and maturity level.

The courts no longer use the financial ability of a parent as a basis for awarding custody. Instead, child support and property distribution awards are used to ensure that the custodial parent has adequate means to financially support the child.

The information sought by the Court in making a custody determination is often introduced through the testimony and reports of child psychologists, social service workers, the law guardian, the parents, witnesses, and the children themselves. Some of the major factors considered by the Court in awarding custody are discussed in more detail below.

A table setting forth criteria commonly used by Courts to determine custody, by state, is set forth at Appendix 1.

### Child's Preference

The courts struggle with the amount of weight to be given a child's preference when it comes to a custody decision. For example, a child may simply prefer to live with the more "lenient" parent, which may not always be in the child's best interests.

The judge will usually meet with the child "in camera"—i.e., in the judge's chambers. The judge will often interview the child privately so that he or she can determine, by experience, whether the child's preference—particularly the very young child—is the result of programming by one parent.

The child's age and maturity are factors to be considered. For example, an older child's preference may be given greater weight. It is recognized that teenagers often make their own custody decisions "with their feet," and it is nearly impossible to force a teenager to stay with one parent against his or her will.

### Religious Issues

There are many contested issues involved in child custody litigation. Reaching a decision may be further complicated when the religious upbringing of the child becomes an issue in the dispute. Controversy over the religious upbringing of a child introduces constitutional considerations into the proceedings. The court is called upon to balance the religious rights of the parents and child, while constrained by the Fourteenth Amendment that makes the First Amendment to the United States Constitution the state judiciary. The First Amendment prohibits the making of law respecting an establishment of religion, or prohibiting its free exercise.

The court is clearly not permitted to favor one religion over another in making a custody determination. However, the court may consider whether a particular religion maintains practices that are harmful to the child. Further, a court may consider whether a particular religion has been an important factor in the child's life, and whether such continuity is in the best interests of the child. This does not require the court to make a value judgment concerning any particular religion.

In general, a custodial parent in a sole custody situation has the right to determine the child's religious upbringing. However, this does not preclude the non-custodial parent from exposing the child to his or her religion, unless there is some indication of harm to the child. This reasoning would likely be followed in joint custody situations where the parents are unable to cooperate in a decision on the child's religious upbringing. Parents may also agree, in writing, as to the religious upbringing of the child.

A sample clause concerning the religious upbringing of a child is set forth at Appendix 2.

### Psychological Evaluation

At the beginning of a custody dispute, the court usually appoints an independent psychologist to assist in determining the custody arrangement. The court-appointed psychologist is not hired by either parent; therefore, his or her recommendation is likely to be impartial.

In addition to a psychological evaluation of the child, the court will often request an evaluation of all persons who participate in the caretaking of the child. This includes the parents, stepparents, and may also include grandparents or other family members who are in close day-to-day contact with the child.

A psychological evaluation may include:

1. testing;

2. behavioral observation;

3. interviews; and

4. an investigation into areas which explore the parent's overall stability, such as the parent's willingness to cooperate with the other parent, his or her relationship to the child, and his or her availability for the child's day-to-day needs, etc.

A review of relevant records, such as school records, police records, medical records, and any past psychological treatment may also be helpful in reaching a determination.

The attorneys for the parents may also bring in their own expert witness psychologist to promote their position and render a second opinion. A parent who disagrees with the recommendations of the court-appointed psychologist will likely bring in his or her own expert to rebut any adverse testimony of the court-appointed psychologist. However, the fact that a litigant compensates the retained expert lessens the impact of the testimony, which is often perceived as biased.

A psychologist is under an ethical duty to avoid situations which involve or give the appearance of a conflict of interest. For example, the court-appointed psychologist owes a duty to the court to render a recommendation that is solely focused on the best interests of the child. If the same psychologist were also the treating therapist for one of the litigants, this would create a dual relationship that would endanger the impartiality of the psychologist in rendering his or her recommendation.

Nevertheless, in the above scenario, once the litigation has been concluded, the dual relationship is ended and the psychologist may take the role as the treating therapist for one or more of the parties. However, he or she is thereafter ethically prohibited from resuming his or her role as the independent evaluator in any future custody litigation involving the same parties.

## TYPES OF CUSTODY ARRANGEMENTS

### In General

There are a number of custody arrangements which the parents can maintain following a divorce. If the parents can amicably agree to work out child custody issues in a reasonable manner, without court intervention, the child will be able to move on with the adjustments that much sooner. Litigation creates a bitter atmosphere and clouds what should truly be the most important issue—the happiness and emotional health of the child.

In the unfortunate event that the parents cannot amicably agree to a reasonable custody arrangement, the dispute must be settled in court. However, custody litigation should be avoided if at all possible, and reserved only for those instances where a child's welfare would be seriously endangered by living with a parent who is clearly unfit.

The three most common types of custody arrangements are: (1) sole custody; (2) joint custody; and (3) split custody.

### Sole Custody

Sole custody exists when one parent is designated the custodial parent—i.e., the parent who takes care of the basic daily needs of the child. The sole custodial parent also has the right to make all of the decisions concerning the child, including those decisions affecting the child's education and health. He or she is under no obligation to consult with the other parent before making such decisions.

In a sole custody situation, the child lives with the custodial parent. Although the non-custodial parent does not relinquish parenthood, his or her role is severely limited and consists mainly of visits with the child. If the non-custodial parent was previously very involved in the child's daily upbringing, sole custody presents a drastic change for both child and parent. Thus, it is important that the non-custodial parent maintain as close a relationship with the child as possible under the circumstances—e.g. regular telephone contact—in order to lessen the emotional impact of such a loss.

### Joint Custody

Joint custody exists when both parents legally share responsibility for the child. Although the living arrangements may be similar to that of a sole custody situation, joint custody implies that both parents are entitled to take equal responsibility for any decisions affecting the child. Such decisions may involve medical, educational and religious issues. Of course, to succeed, the parties to the joint custody arrangement must be able to cooperate with each other.

In working out a joint custody arrangement, efforts may be made to more evenly divide the child's time with each parent. For example, the child may be in the physical custody of the mother during weekdays and in the physical custody of the father during weekends, or the child may spend alternating weeks with each parent.

For an example of joint custody scheduling, see the sample joint custody agreement set forth in the Appendix 3.

In some situations, it is the parents who agree to "move" in and out of the house, and the child maintains his or her residence in the former marital home. In this way, the child's life is not as severely disrupted as a result of the differences that separated the adults.

In any event, there are a variety of ways in which living arrangements can be worked out as long as the parents are dedicated to making joint custody work. Of course, such a schedule also necessitates that the parents live within a reasonable distance from each other.

The ability of the parents to cooperate with each other is a priority consideration of the court in granting joint custody. If the parents are unable to put their differences aside and recognize that it is the child's best interests that must remain in the forefront, a joint custody arrangement simply will not work.

### Split Custody

In families where there is more than one child, split custody may be an alternative—i.e., each party may take custody of one or more of the children. For example, the boys may live primarily with the father, and the girls may live primarily with the mother.

However, courts are generally not in favor of splitting up siblings, based on a general belief that it is best for children of the same family to grow up together. This is particularly so following a divorce, because siblings can be a great source of stability and comfort to one another.

Although sibling splitting is generally discouraged, split custody may be awarded when it is in a child's best interests. This may occur when the children have developed separate and distinct parental attachments, or where it is clearly one child's preference to be with the "other" parent.

## MODIFICATION OF A CUSTODY ORDER

Parents may agree to modify the terms of any custody or visitation order. They can do so even after a final divorce decree is filed with the court. This can be accomplished without a court order; however, it is advisable to have the court enforce the modification to ensure its enforceability. If one parent wants to modify a custody or visitation order, but the other parent refuses, a motion must be filed with the court seeking modification of the court order. The grounds for modification are usually "a substantial change in circumstances" since the original order was made. However, the court will still want to make sure the "best interests of the child" standard is followed when modifying the original order.

Examples of a change in circumstances may include:

1. A substantial change in the other parent's lifestyle that threatens or harms the child, e.g., the custodial parent has become alcohol or drug-dependent.

2. A significant geographical move by the custodial parent that threatens to disrupt the non-custodial parent's right of visitation.

3. A devastating event in the custodial home, e.g., sexual molestation of the child by a stepparent.

In addition, the custodial parent may request a temporary modification of custody under certain circumstances, e.g., for an extended hospital stay. In this case, physical custody would be restored once the custodial parent is discharged from the hospital and again able to care for the child.

## CUSTODY RIGHTS OF MINOR PARENTS

### In General

Becoming a parent does not emancipate a minor for all purposes. If a minor is not self-supportive, and does not live independently of his or her parents, the minor is not considered emancipated, whether or not they are a parent. Nevertheless, minors do acquire some of the rights of adults when they have a child.

For example, minor parents have the right to custody of their child and to make decisions regarding the child's upbringing, such as consenting to medical treatment, educational planning, and adoption. Minor parents maintain these rights regardless of whether they live with their own parents or not, as long as they adequately care for their child.

### The Right to Consent to Adoption

Teenage parents can generally consent to the adoption of their child without their own parents' consent. If the father is not married to the mother—known as a "putative father"—he can generally sign a consent form to have the baby adopted at any time. However, the mother typically must wait until after the baby is born to sign the consent form and relinquish her parental rights.

To be valid, the consent must be "voluntary, intelligent, and deliberate," which means that the consent must not be forced or accepted without presenting the mother with sufficient information about what termination of parental rights will mean, and what alternatives and services exist for teen parents. Thus, the minor's parents cannot force the minor to place the baby for adoption. The law may require that the minor's parents be notified of the hearing at which the minor's parental rights will be terminated.

## CUSTODY RIGHTS OF UNMARRIED PARENTS

### In General

Many unmarried couples today choose to have children out of wedlock, or to adopt a child. In general, unmarried parents have the same legal rights and responsibilities with respect to their children as do married parents. Nevertheless, there are some legal and practical issues an unmarried couple may face when raising children, which are discussed below.

### The Adoptive Child

Although many states permit an unmarried couple to adopt a child, the agencies involved in approving such adoptions are often reluctant to place a child for adoption with unmarried prospective parents. The concern is the stability of the unmarried couple who are legally able to marry yet choose not to do so. Although this may appear to be a discriminatory practice, it is an obstacle the unmarried couple must face when trying to adopt.

If an adoption is approved, both parents will be considered the adopted child's legal parents, and they will be responsible for raising and supporting the adopted child. In addition, as with a biological child, if the married couple separates, each parent has an equal legal right to seek custody, visitation and child support for the adopted child.

### The Co-Parenting Agreement

A non-legal parent who wants to have parental rights and responsibilities for their partner's child are advised to execute a co-parenting agreement, which should be signed by both parties and notarized. The co-parenting agreement may contain some or all of the following provisions:

1. An agreement to share parental responsibilities, including the obligation to provide support to the child;

2. An agreement as to custody and visitation should the couple separate;

3. A provision authorizing the non-legal parent to consent to medical care for the child;

4. A stipulation that the child will be named as a beneficiary in both the legal parent and non-legal parent's will.

5. A stipulation that both the legal parent and the non-legal parent will name the other as the child's guardian in his or her will. Nevertheless, if there is a surviving legal or biological parent, or another close relative who petitions for custody if the legal parent passes away, this provision is not legally binding and may not be upheld by a court.

A sample co-parenting agreement is set forth at Appendix 4.

## CUSTODY RIGHTS OF SAME-SEX PARENTS

### In General

Courts have recently been asked to rule upon the custody and visitation rights of same-sex parents following the breakup of the couple. In 2006, the California Supreme Court became the first court in the nation to rule that gay and lesbian partners who raise a child together in a family setting should be considered legal parents after their breakup, with the same rights and responsibilities as heterosexual parents, regardless of marital status or biological connection with the child.

Although courts in other states have granted visitation and other parental rights to same-sex partners who had bonded with their child even if not biologically related to the child ("psychological parent"), those rulings did not recognize complete parental status. The California ruling established full parent-child relationships, which would include such rights as inheritance, Social Security and health insurance coverage for children, as well as custody and visitation for parents.

In its ruling, the court noted that the both parents were legal parents which entitled them to visitation, even over the objections of the former partner and biological parent of the child. The court also ruled that the non-custodial parent was also required to pay child support.

### The American Academy of Pediatrics (AAP)

Although this subject is still controversial, same-sex parents have gained support from the American Academy of Pediatrics (AAP) which opines that children who are born to, or adopted by, one member of a gay or lesbian couple deserve the security of two legally recognized parents. The AAP released a policy statement on this topic that suggests children with parents who are homosexual have the same advantages and the same expectations for health, adjustment and development as children whose parents are heterosexual.

According to the policy statement, co-parenting in a same-sex relationship provides for the following:

1. Guarantees that the second parent's custody rights will be protected if the first parent falls ill or dies.

2. Protects the second parent's rights to custody and visitation if the couple separates.

3. Establishes the requirement for child support from both parents in the event of the parents' separation.

4. Ensures the child's eligibility for health benefits from both parents.

5. Provides legal grounds for either parent to provide consent for medical care and other important decisions.

6. Creates the basis for financial security for children by ensuring eligibility to all appropriate entitlements, such as Social Security survivor's benefits.

### Rights of Gay and Lesbian Parents Following Heterosexual Divorce

Many parents have produced children during a heterosexual marriage, and subsequently pursued a gay or lesbian lifestyle following divorce. Courts have been split over the custody and/or visitation rights of the gay or lesbian parent. Many courts have chosen to deny a gay parent's custody petition, or place strict limitations on any visitation with their child, particularly if the child would be subjected to the alternate lifestyle during visits.

In a few states, a parent's sexual orientation is not supposed to prevent that parent from being awarded custody. State appellate courts have ruled that sexual orientation of a parent is not a factor in determining custody unless it is demonstrated to actually harm the child. However, many judges opposed to this lifestyle may still find reasons other than the parent's sexual orientation to deny custody to a gay or lesbian parent, and their views reflected in their custody rulings.

In addition, a small number of courts strongly oppose granting custody or visitation rights to a gay or lesbian parent, and rely on state sodomy laws to underscore their rulings in this regard.

A table of state custody cases involving same-sex partners is set forth at Appendix 5.

# CHAPTER 3:
# VISITATION

**THE NON-CUSTODIAL PARENT'S RIGHT TO VISITATION**

When one parent is designated the primary physical custodian of the child, the other parent—the "non-custodial parent"—is given what is commonly known as "visitation" rights. Unless the parents are so co-operative that they are able to enjoy flexible visitation "as the parties may agree," the court will order a visitation schedule, which may be quite detailed.

**SCHEDULING VISITATION**

### In General

A visitation schedule is usually ordered even when joint custody is awarded. However, the schedule is usually worded so as to avoid making one parent feel like a "visitor." The schedule is often written in terms detailing which parent will have "physical custody" of the child on such and such dates. The court usually orders visitation to take place at reasonable times and places, allowing the parents to exercise flexibility by taking into consideration both the parents' and the child's schedules.

For the reasonable visitation approach to succeed, however, the parents must cooperate and communicate with each other frequently. Ideally, the parents should be able to work out a suitable and mutually convenient visitation schedule without court intervention. Unfortunately, this is often not the case, particularly in situations following a bitter divorce. Parents bent on disagreement often argue about the most minute details of the visitation schedule, e.g., pick-up and drop-off times.

### Court-Ordered Fixed Visitation Schedule

In those situations where the parents clearly cannot agree, the court is called upon to order a fixed visitation schedule, particularly if there is so much bitterness and hostility between the parents that constant contact between them may be detrimental to the child. The order will often detail exact dates, times, and locations for weekly, holiday and vacation visitation to take place.

### Supervised Visitation

If a non-custodial parent has a history of violent, destructive, or dangerous behavior—e.g., abuse, alcoholism, drug use, etc.—the court will usually require supervised visitation with the child. This means that visitation between the parent and child can only take place if another adult is present during the visit. The supervising adult does not have to be someone the child knows, but is usually a person agreed upon between the parents and approved by the court.

### Transportation Obligations

When working out a visitation schedule, one issue that must be addressed is the child's transportation to and from the non-custodial parent's home. In many cases, the time and cost of transportation is shared between the parents. However, if the parents live far apart, the parent who is most able to pay the cost of transportation generally agrees to do so.

Oftentimes, following a divorce, the parents cannot agree on transportation obligations and costs, and the Court must step in and include transportation arrangements in the visitation order, taking into consideration each party's financial circumstances, and any other relevant factors.

### Age as a Factor in Determining Visitation Schedule

The length and frequency of visitation with the non-custodial parent is often dependent upon, among other factors, the age the child. The general consensus is that children under five years of age are best suited to consistent, frequent visits with the non-custodial parent, particularly when the child has strongly bonded with the parent.

It has been suggested, however, that the younger child preferably maintain the consistency of sleeping in his or her own crib until approximately two years of age, in order to make the child feel more secure in his or her surroundings. As the child matures, overnight visits can be introduced at longer and more frequent intervals.

School-age children usually participate in extracurricular activities and develop friendships among their peers. At this age, a balance must be reached between allowing the child to maintain a normal social life versus "sticking to" the visitation schedule. Flexibility is often the preferred route to take to avoid putting pressure on the child to "make the choice." Parents who are able to cooperate with each other will likely be able to work around an active child's schedule. It is important, however, to maintain consistent telephone contact when physical visitation is limited.

Once a child reaches adolescence, given the likelihood of a very active social life, it is unlikely that any scheduled visitation will work if it interferes with their plans. Again, flexibility, an "open-door policy," and frequent telephone contact will help to maintain a strong parent-child bond.

### Relocation of Custodial Parent

In almost all cases, the non-custodial parent has an absolute right to visitation with the child. Only in situations where the non-custodial parent is clearly a danger to the child will the court attempt to curtail the visitation rights of the non-custodial parent. In addition, attempts by the custodial parent to move the child out of the jurisdiction, thereby cutting off the non-custodial parent's visitation rights, will be seriously scrutinized by the court. The relationship between the non-custodial parent and the child is a very important factor in the court's determination.

Many jurisdictions require court approval before allowing the custodial parent to move the child out of the jurisdiction, and often will not allow such removal unless there is sufficient justification for the move, such as remarriage. Of course, the court cannot restrict the relocation of the custodial parent, but it can transfer custody of the child to the non-custodial parent if the custodial parent insists on relocating. If the custody agreement restricts relocation, the court will most likely uphold the terms of the agreement. The courts generally hold that continued contact with both parents is in the best interests of the child and should be maintained.

## VISITATION RIGHTS OF THIRD PARTIES

### In General

Children form strong bonds with many people during the course of their lives. When their family unit is disrupted, either by divorce or death, their relationship with various other family members is also radically altered. Thus, it is important for parents to recognize that depriving a child of a physically and emotionally close relationship may be detrimental to the child. It is an additional loss that the child must suffer at an unstable time in their life, when the child is already vulnerable.

Every effort should be made to allow the child to maintain these significant relationships. Although this may be at times inconvenient or undesirable, one must remember that it is not the child's fault that the adults are unable to work out their differences. Following this reasoning, there has been a trend among the states to allow third-party visitation following a divorce or the death of a parent.

A table setting forth third party statutory visitation rights, by state, is set forth at Appendix 6.

### Visitation Rights of a Non-Legal Parent

Both married and unmarried couples may have children living in the home that are not the legal or biological child of one of the partners, such as a stepchild or the child of an unmarried partner. Yet, in long-term relationships, the child and the non-legal parent, who may have lived together for many years, have nevertheless developed a strong parent-child bond. Unfortunately, if the couple separates, the non-legal parent may have no legal right to have any further contact with the child, which is often a very painful experience for both the non-legal parent and the child.

If the couple recognizes the importance of maintaining consistency in the child's life, and wants to avoid the inevitable pain of separation from an important parental figure, they will agree, in writing, to allow the non-legal parent to continue to play a role in the child's life, including the right to visitation. The provisions may be contained in a co-parenting agreement, as discussed in Chapter 2 of this almanac.

If the couple separates without making such a written agreement, the non-legal parent will generally have to petition a court for visitation rights. In general, the non-legal parent has no legal rights to custody of, or visitation with, the child, and historically, courts have denied custody and visitation petitions brought on behalf of a non-legal parent.

However, as discussed in Chapter 2, in recent years, some courts have recognized that maintaining a relationship with a parental figure, particularly when there has been a long-term, significant parent/child connection, may be in the best interests of the child, and have awarded visitation to those parents deemed "psychological" or "equitable" parents.

The reader is advised to check the law of his or her own jurisdiction concerning the custody and visitation rights of non-legal parents.

### Grandparent Visitation

In addition to a parental figure, children also form many close relationships with their extended family members, such as aunts, uncles, cousins, stepsiblings, etc. The most significant of such relationships is often the child's grandparents. It has been recognized that grandparents play a very important role in a child's development.

When parents separate or divorce, grandparents' relationships with their grandchildren are often in jeopardy, thus, all states have enacted laws which allow grandparents to seek visitation rights with their grandchildren after divorce or separation. In fact, grandparents have the legal right to petition a court for visitation privileges with their grandchildren even when both parents of the child object to the visitation or when the child's parents are still together.

If the parents are divorced, it is important that the grandparent does not take an active role in the dispute between the parents. This may be difficult because the grandparent will understandably be concerned about his or her own child. However, if the grandparent is to play a positive role in the child's life, particularly during a difficult divorce, it is crucial that he or she remain impartial and avoid involving the child in the dispute. Any negative views the grandparent may hold about the other parent should not be shared with the child or the grandparent may risk losing visitation privileges.

Some of the factors courts consider in awarding visitation privileges to a grandparent include:

1. the nature of the existing relationship between the grandparent and child;

2. the effect of such visitation on the child's relationship with his or her parents;

3. the child's wishes in maintaining a relationship with his or her grandparent; and

4. the effect of such visitation on the child's emotional development.

A table of state statutes governing grandparent visitation is set forth at Appendix 7, and the American Bar Association Policy Resolution on Grandparent Visitation is set forth at Appendix 8.

# CHAPTER 4:
# CUSTODIAL INTERFERENCE

## IN GENERAL

In most states, it is against the law to keep a child from his or her parent or legal guardian with the intent of depriving that person of custody, even if the person who takes the child also has custodial rights. This is known as custodial interference. Custodial interference may occur, for example, if the custodial parent absconds with the child with the intent of depriving the non-custodial parent from exercising his or her visitation rights, or if the non-custodial parent fails to return the child to the custodial parent following visitation.

In many states, if the child is taken out-of-state, it is a felony. A good faith defense may apply, however, if the parent absconds with the child in order to prevent imminent bodily harm to the child, e.g., physical abuse or sexual molestation.

A custodial parent may also interfere with the non-custodial parents right to visitation by making visitation impossible. For example, some custodial parents make constant excuses to avoid surrendering the child for scheduled visits, e.g., by claiming the child is sick, etc. If the custodial parent maliciously or willfully interferes with the non-custodial parent's visitation rights, some jurisdictions will use this interference as a basis to transfer physical custody to the other parent.

EXAMPLE:

FATHER and MOTHER divorce and MOTHER is awarded custody of SON. FATHER is awarded liberal visitation rights according to an explicit schedule, which includes every other weekend, certain holidays, Father's Day, and one half of the summer and winter vacations. FATHER subsequently remarries. MOTHER does not want SON to visit FATHER and his new wife. Every time FATHER arrives to pick up SON as scheduled, MOTHER comes up with an excuse why FATHER cannot visit with SON. This goes on for several months, until FATHER petitions the court to enforce his visitation rights. When FATHER arrives to retrieve SON for his scheduled visitation during summer vacation, he finds that MOTHER has maliciously taken SON out of state to visit her relatives. FATHER petitions the Court for a change in custody.

POSSIBLE OUTCOME:

> The court may transfer physical custody to FATHER because of MOTHER'S willful and malicious violation of FATHER'S legal right to visitation with SON.

## INTERSTATE CUSTODY LITIGATION

A parent may be confronted with having to deal with child custody issues across state lines. These issues usually arise when the custodial parent relocates out-of-state in defiance of a court order. As the "missing children" hotlines and milk carton advertisements demonstrate, a significant number of parents choose to flee with their children rather than allow the courts to determine custody.

A parent often removes a child and drops out of sight completely. Of course, this causes the abandoned parent immense pain and suffering, as well as the financial burden of trying to locate the child and/or litigate custody issues in another state.

### Forum Shopping

It is often the absconding parent's intention to relocate in a jurisdiction which he or she feels will render a more favorable determination than would have been made in the child's home state. Of course, this also creates an extreme financial hardship and disadvantage for the other parent who must litigate custody in a distant jurisdiction.

Full faith and credit is a legal principle that requires the court of one state to recognize and enforce valid orders and judgments made by the court of another state. Unfortunately, states often refused to afford full faith and credit to a custody order made by the courts of another state, and would instead make their own custody award. This led to conflicting custody orders, and children would be kidnapped and shuffled back and forth between the two states by the parent wishing to enforce the custody order that was favorable to them in their own state.

As discussed below, two important pieces of legislation—the Uniform Child Custody Jurisdiction Act (UCCJA) and the Parental Kidnapping Prevention Act (PKPA)—were enacted to combat this serious problem of jurisdictional conflict and parental forum shopping in custody decisions. In fact, the UCCJA now requires states to give full faith and credit to the custody orders of other states.

### The Uniform Child Custody Jurisdiction Act

The Uniform Child Custody Jurisdiction Act of 1968 (UCCJA) has been adopted by all of the states and the District of Columbia. The UCCJA's goal is to eliminate the motives for forum shopping among the states, and to encourage cooperation between state courts. The UCCJA favors awarding jurisdiction to the child's home state, thus deterring parental forum shopping and child snatching. Further, the UCCJA prohibits a state from exercising jurisdiction in a custody action if another state's court has already been involved in the case.

When the courts of two states are in conflict, the UCCJA provides that a federal court can rule as to which state is the proper forum in which to litigate custody. The federal court will not, however, decide the merits of a custody dispute. The UCCJA requires both jurisdictions to cooperate in determining the proper forum in which to resolve the custody dispute.

The UCCJA sets forth the standards a particular jurisdiction must meet in order to make a custody determination when two states are involved, in order of preference, as follows:

1. Home State—The state is the child's home state, i.e., the child has resided in the state for the six previous months, or was residing in the state but is absent because a parent has removed the child from or retained the child outside of the state.

2. Significant Connection—There are significant connections with people, such as grandparents and extended family members, in the state, as well as substantial evidence that the child's care, protection, training, and personal relationships are in the state.

3. Emergency—The child is in the state and either has been abandoned or is in danger of being abused or neglected if sent back to the other state.

4. Vacuum—No other state can meet one of the above three tests, or a state can meet at least one of the tests but has declined to make a custody decision.

If a state cannot meet one of the foregoing tests, the courts of that state cannot make a custody award even if the child is present in the state. In addition, if a parent has wrongfully removed a child to, or retained a child in particular state, in order for that state to meet one of the foregoing conditions—e.g., the parent attempts to create a "home state" or establish "significant connections" in that state—that parent will be denied custody.

If more than one state meets the foregoing standards, the law requires that only one state award custody. Thus, once the first state makes a custody award, another state can neither make a conflicting award, nor modify the existing order.

The Uniform Child Custody Jurisdiction Act is set forth at Appendix 9.

### The Parental Kidnapping Prevention Act

The Parental Kidnapping Prevention Act of 1980 (PKPA) requires the appropriate authorities of every state to enforce custody and visitation orders made by courts having proper jurisdiction. The PKPA also authorizes the Federal Parental Locator Service to locate children who have been abducted by a parent. Thus, when a parent removes a child from a jurisdiction against court order or contrary to a custody agreement, the lawful custodial parent can obtain federal assistance in locating the child.

In many jurisdictions, the parent who wrongfully takes the child is subject to criminal sanctions for absconding with the child and interfering with custody. Under the PKPA, the Fugitive Felon Act applies to state felony cases involving parental kidnapping and interstate or international flight to avoid prosecution. In such a case, a request for a federal Unlawful Flight to Avoid Prosecution (UFAP) warrant may be filed with the local U.S. Attorney's Office by the state prosecutor.

Relevant provisions of The Parental Kidnapping Act are set forth at Appendix 10.

### The Uniform Child-Custody Jurisdiction and Enforcement Act (UCCJEA)

The Uniform Child-Custody Jurisdiction and Enforcement Act (UCCJEA) is a uniform State law that was approved in 1997 by the National Conference of Commissioners on Uniform State Laws (NCCUSL) to replace its 1968 Uniform Child Custody Jurisdiction Act (UCCJA), discussed above. The NCCUSL drafts and proposes laws in areas where it believes uniformity is important, but the laws become effective only upon adoption by state legislatures. As of July 2005, the Act has been enacted by 40 states and the District of Columbia.

A list of jurisdictions that have enacted the Uniform Child-Custody Jurisdiction and Enforcement Act (UCCJEA) is set forth at Appendix 11.

The UCCJEA is designed to deter interstate parental kidnapping and to promote uniform jurisdiction and enforcement provisions in interstate child-custody and visitation cases. The UCCJEA is not a substantive custody statute. It does not dictate standards for making or modifying child custody and visitation decisions; instead, it determines which States' courts have and should exercise jurisdiction to do so.

The UCCJEA is intended to be a complete replacement for the UCCJA in those states that adopt the Act. Articles 1 and 2 of the UCCJEA contain jurisdictional rules that essentially bring the UCCJA into conformity with the PKPA. Modeling the UCCJEA's jurisdictional standards on the PKPA's standards is intended to produce custody determinations that are entitled under Federal law to full faith and credit in sister States. Under articles 1 and 2, the UCCJEA, among other things:

1. Applies to a range of proceedings in which custody or visitation is at issue.

2. Grants priority to home state jurisdiction;

3. Preserves exclusive, continuing jurisdiction in the decree state if that state determines that it has a basis for exercising jurisdiction. Such jurisdiction continues until the child, his or her parents, and any person acting as the child's parent move away from the decree State.

4. Authorizes courts to exercise emergency jurisdiction in cases involving family abuse and limits the relief available in emergency cases to temporary custody orders.

5. Revamps the rules governing inconvenient forum analysis, requiring courts to consider specified factors.

6. Directs courts to decline jurisdiction created by unjustifiable conduct.

The UCCJEA also establishes uniform procedures for interstate enforcement of child custody and visitation determinations. In particular, Article 3 of the UCCJEA:

1. Authorizes temporary enforcement of visitation determinations.

2. Creates an interstate registration process for out-of-State custody determinations

3. Establishes a procedure for speedy interstate enforcement of custody and visitation determinations.

4. Authorizes issuance of warrants directing law enforcement to pick up children at risk of being removed from the State.

5. Authorizes public officials to assist in the civil enforcement of custody determinations and in Hague Convention cases.

The UCCJEA applies to a variety of proceedings. Specifically, courts in UCCJEA States must comply with the statute when custody and visitation issues arise in proceedings for divorce, separation, neglect, abuse, dependency, guardianship, paternity, termination of parental rights, and protection from domestic violence.

A sample petition seeking custody or visitation pursuant to the UCCJEA is set forth at Appendix 12.

### Parenting Across State Lines

Once jurisdiction has been established in another state, the non-custodial parent necessarily suffers a type of forced exile from his or her child. In those cases, the courts often attempt to fashion a remedy that will assist the non-custodial parent in maintaining a meaningful relationship with the child.

For example, the non-custodial parent may be awarded expanded visitation privileges, such as more holiday visits, or entire summers, etc. This expansion of visitation is crucial to maintain a strong parent-child bond, particularly because visits during the school year will necessarily be limited if there is a significant distance between the custodial and non-custodial homes.

## INTERNATIONAL CUSTODY LITIGATION

### In General

International parental child abduction has become a serious problem in the last several decades. This is due in large part to the relative ease of international travel, and the increase in cross-cultural marriages. The outcome of a custody dispute that crosses international boundaries depends largely on the country to which the parent relocates. The parent left behind must deal with the complexities of foreign law, and the large expense of having to litigate a custody case in a foreign country, where he or she may be confronted with cultural bias favoring the absconding parent with close ties to the country.

### Precautions

If you are in a cross-cultural marriage, and fear that your child is vulnerable to abduction, there are a number of precautions you should take. You should be aware that a child is particularly vulnerable if there is trouble in the marriage, or an impending divorce, and the other parent has close ties with a foreign country.

In order to prepare for the possibility of an abduction, the United States Department of State has suggested the following precautions:

1. Realize that voluntary travel to the foreign country may result in your child being prevented from returning to the United States. In fact, some foreign countries not only prohibit travel by a child, but also a woman, without the husband's permission. Thus, it is crucial that you inquire about all of the applicable laws and cultural traditions before traveling to a foreign country.

2. Compile information about the other parent to be used in case of an abduction. Keep names and addresses of friends and relatives in the United States and in the foreign country. Maintain a record of the other parent's personal data, such as passport number, social security number, and driver's license number, etc.

3. Keep an up-to-date written and detailed description of your child and take color photographs every six months. This information will be very helpful in locating the child if the need should arise.

4. Teach your child what to do in case he or she is removed from the country. For example, teach your child how to use a telephone to call for help.

5. If you are separated or divorced, it is best to obtain a custody decree that incorporates a provision prohibiting your child from traveling out of the United States without your permission. Provide certified copies of the decree to anybody who may be responsible for your child, such as the school, daycare center, camp, and babysitter, etc. Alert them to the possibility that an abduction may take place and instruct them to contact you if there are any unscheduled attempts to retrieve your child.

### THE HAGUE CONVENTION ON THE CIVIL ASPECTS OF INTERNATIONAL CHILD ABDUCTION

#### In General

The Hague Convention on the Civil Aspects of International Child Abduction (the "Hague Convention"), adopted by the Hague Conference in 1980, has attempted to combat the problem of international parental child abduction. The Hague Convention's objective is to resolve problems related to international parental child abduction among its member nations by making sure such children are immediately returned to their country of origin. The member nations are referred to in the Convention as "contracting states."

The Hague Convention is set forth at Appendix 13.

#### Parties to the Hague Convention

In 1988, the United States became a party to the Hague Convention, and implemented legislation providing for the commencement of international child custody litigation under federal law. Its provisions largely mirror the UCCJA and provide procedures for filing international petitions seeking the return of a child, visitation rights, and habeas corpus proceedings. As of 2005, 58 countries had become parties to the Hague Convention.

A list of parties to the Hague Convention and their date of entry is set forth at Appendix 14.

### Central Authorities

As set forth in Article 6 of the Hague Convention, each contracting state must designate a Central Authority to handle complaints of child abduction, and to cooperate with the Central Authorities of other contracting states to carry out the objectives of the Convention, i.e., secure the prompt return of abducted children. The duties of the Central Authorities in carrying out this objective include:

1. Discovering the whereabouts of the abducted child;

2. Taking such measures necessary to prevent further harm to the child;

3. Securing the voluntary return of the child and amicably resolving the issues;

4. Exchanging information concerning the child;

5. Providing general information concerning its own law as it pertains to the Convention;

6. Initiating judicial or administrative proceedings necessary to secure the return of the child;

7. Providing legal aid and advice to the parties;

8. Providing administrative arrangements necessary to secure the return of the child; and

9. Keeping each other informed and eliminating obstacles that would hinder carrying out the objective of the Convention.

A list Central Authorities and their websites is set forth at Appendix 15.

### Office of Children's Issues (CI)

If you suspect that your child has been abducted to a country that is a party to the Hague Convention, you should contact the Office of Children's Issues (CI), an office of the Overseas Citizens Services (OCS) in the U.S. Department of State. CI works closely with parents, attorneys, other government agencies, and private organizations in the U.S. to prevent international abductions. CI has been designated by Congress as the Central Authority to administer the Hague Convention in the United States.

The Office of Children's Issues can be reached at the following:

U.S. Department of State
Overseas Citizens Services
Office of Children's Issues
2201 C Street NW
Washington, DC 20520
Tel: 1-888-407-4747
Tel: 202-501-4444 (from overseas)

**Abduction to Non-Hague Convention Member Countries**

If the foreign country to which your child is abducted is not a party to the Hague Convention, you can seek legal remedies against the absconding parent in the federal civil and criminal court systems. Once you suspect that an abduction has occurred, there are a number of steps you can take to locate your child and press charges against the abducting parent:

1. If you have not already done so, seek a custody decree that prohibits your child from traveling without your permission. Without a custody decree granting you sole custody of the child, you will not have legal standing to bring an action.

2. File a missing person report with the local police department and the National Center for Missing and Exploited Children, and request that the Federal Parent Locator Service attempt a search for the absconding parent.

3. Request the Department of State, Overseas Citizens Services, Office of Children's Issues (CI) to initiate a welfare and whereabouts search for your child overseas.

4. Inform the embassy and consulates of the country to which you suspect your child has been taken of your custody decree. Instruct them not to issue a foreign passport or visa to your child.

5. Check the U.S. Passport Agency to see whether a passport has been issued in your child's name.

6. If your child is school age, contact his or her school officials and ask to be informed if anyone requests a transfer of your child's records.

7. Try and track down the absconding parent through personal contacts and records, e.g., friends and relatives, and credit card and telephone bills.

8. Once your child has been located, retain an attorney in the foreign jurisdiction.

9. Seek to have an arrest warrant under state and/or federal statutes issued for the arrest of the absconding parent.

10. Once the arrest warrant has been issued, have the absconding parent's name registered with the National Crime Information Center (NCIS) and, if a U.S. citizen, seek to have his or her passport revoked. Consider whether extradition would be possible.

# CHAPTER 5:
# CHILD SUPPORT

## IN GENERAL

Child support is the payment of money from one parent to another for the maintenance of the child of the relationship, whether or not the parties to the relationship were ever married. The amount of child support can be agreed upon by the parties, as long as the custodial parent—the primary caretaker with whom the child legally resides—is made aware of the amount the child may be entitled to under the Federal Child Support Guidelines, as discussed below. In addition, the agreement must be fair to all parties and in the best interests of the child. Upon application to the appropriate court, the parties can have the child support agreement converted into an enforceable legal order.

Because the payment of child support is generally made to the custodial parent by the non-custodial parent, physical custody of the child is often a "sticking point" in reaching a custody agreement. In many cases, custody litigation begins after the parties are unable to agree on child support issues

## ESTABLISHING THE SUPPORT ORDER

If the parties cannot agree to a child support amount, the decision will be made by the court after a formal hearing. Most states use administrative procedures to expedite the establishment of a legally binding support order. If the parents of the child for whom child support is sought were never married, the paternity of the child must be established before an order of support can be made.

Establishing paternity is discussed more fully in Chapter 7 of this almanac.

### Modification of a Support Order

Depending on the laws of the particular state, support awards can be increased or decreased if one of the parties seeks modification of the order. The ability to modify a support order depends on certain factors, as set forth by the state, which may include a change in circumstances of the parties, such as a loss of employment, or a change in the needs of the child.

### Federal Child Support Guidelines

In 1989, the federal government enacted child support guidelines. All states are required to use the guidelines when determining the amount of a child support award where the parties cannot mutually agree to a support amount. The guidelines set forth a formula, based on such factors as parental income and the number of children for whom support is sought, in order to arrive at the support amount.

The federal child support guidelines must be used unless it can be shown that to use them would be unjust or inappropriate in a particular case. If a court departs from using the guidelines in any case, it must give its reasons, on the record, for its decision.

A Child Support Worksheet is set forth at Appendix 16.

If the non-custodial parent is employed and covered by health insurance through his or her employer, the Court may also order the health plan administrator to enroll the child in the health plan and provide the custodial parent with identification cards and other information necessary to access the health care coverage. A certified copy of this signed order must generally be served on the employer of the person legally responsible to provide health insurance.

A sample Qualified Medical Child Support Order is set forth at Appendix 17.

## CHILD SUPPORT ENFORCEMENT

### Federal Initiatives

In recognition of the need for strict enforcement of child support orders, the federal government has implemented a variety of initiatives for the collection of child support, and all states are obligated to follow federal directives regarding child support enforcement. In addition, the federal government requires the states to implement enforcement programs to ensure that child support payments are made.

A child support enforcement program assists the custodial parent in establishing paternity; establishing a support order; locating a non-paying parent; and collecting and enforcing the child support order. The child support enforcement program is usually handled by the state's child support enforcement office in conjunction with the domestic relations or family court of the jurisdiction.

### Income Deduction Order

All child support orders are subject to immediate wage withholding unless both parents and/or the court agree to a different plan. Thus, the court may direct an employer to automatically deduct the child support payments from the non-custodial parent's wages through the use of an Income Deduction Order. The child support payment is then sent directly to the custodial parent, or to an agency responsible for collecting and disbursing the payments. A non-custodial parent can also request his or her employer to make automatic payroll deductions for child support, and the employer is required, under federal law, to comply with this request

A sample Income Deduction Order is set forth at Appendix 18.

Nevertheless, an Income Deduction Order can only be used when the non-custodial parent is a salaried employee. When the non-custodial parent is self-employed, or otherwise not easily subject to wage withholding, and reneges on his or her obligation to pay child support, other enforcement action can be taken. Such action may include placing liens on the non-custodial parent's real or personal property, or intercepting their federal or state income tax refunds. In addition, child support arrears may also be reported to consumer credit agencies.

### Interstate Child Support Enforcement Legislation

States are also required to vigorously pursue the enforcement of child support orders against out-of-state non-custodial parents. Each state has its own form of interstate enforcement legislation, such as the Uniform Reciprocal Enforcement of Support Act (URESA), which provides for the enforcement of support orders across state lines.

### Federal and State Parent Locator Services

The federal government has established the Federal Parent Locator Service (FPLS), which uses information contained in federal records, such as Internal Revenue Service files, Social Security Administration files, and Veterans Administration files, to locate absent parents. In addition, each state has established a State Parent Locator Services (SPLS), which uses state records, such as Department of Motor Vehicles files and state unemployment insurance files, to locate absent parents.

## TAX ASPECTS OF CHILD SUPPORT

### In General

Child support is not considered income to the parent who receives the payments and is not deductible from the taxable income of the paying parent. In order to claim a child as a dependent, a parent must contribute more than fifty percent of the child's total support. Generally, the custodial parent may claim the exemption. However, the parents may agree otherwise. If the custodial parent assigns the exemption, in writing, to the non-custodial parent, the non-custodial parent can claim the exemption on his or her tax return.

### Tax Benefits

In addition, the following tax benefits are available to parents to offset the cost of raising children:

1. earned income credit;

2. child care credit;

3. medical expense deductions; and

4. head of household filing status.

#### Child Care Tax Credit

The child care tax credit is only available to the custodial parent. In addition, employed custodial parents of a dependent child under the age of 13 are eligible for the credit for child care expenses incurred so that the parent can earn an income. As the custodial parent's income increases, however, the credit phases out.

#### Medical Expenses Deduction

Both the custodial and non-custodial parent can claim a deduction for medical expenses he or she actually paid, but only if those medical expenses exceed a certain percentage of their adjusted gross income. Thus, if the child's total medical expenses are high enough, it may be prudent to allocate them to the lower wage earner so that that parent can take the deduction.

#### Head of Household Filing Status

The "head of household" filing status is only available to the custodial parent who has physical custody of the child more than half of the time. If the parents have joint legal and physical custody, and physical custody is divided evenly between them, neither parent can file as head of household because the dependent child resides with neither parent for more than 50% of the year.

If you have more than one minor child and share joint physical custody, it may be possible to specify your arrangement as 51% physical custody for one child with one parent, and 51% physical custody for the other child with the other parent. Because each parent will then have a dependent child in the home more than 50% of the year, each parent can file as head of household.

## EFFECT OF EMANCIPATION ON CHILD SUPPORT OBLIGATION

The payment of child support is a legal obligation which continues until either the child is emancipated or the paying parent dies. Emancipation occurs when the child reaches the age of majority, which is eighteen. In a few states, such as New York, the obligation to pay child support extends until the child reaches the age of twenty-one.

A child may be also emancipated if he or she marries, joins the armed services, or otherwise voluntarily leaves the care and control of the custodial parent. However, emancipation does not necessarily occur just because a child physically leaves the custodial parent's household, such as for the purpose of attending school.

EXAMPLE:

FATHER and MOTHER divorce and MOTHER is awarded custody of, and child support for, their 17-year-old son. They live in New York, where the age of majority is 21. When SON turns 18, he enlists in the United States Marine Corps. FATHER stops paying child support to MOTHER under the doctrine of emancipation. MOTHER petitions the court requesting an order that FATHER pay child support because SON has not yet reached the age of 21.

POSSIBLE OUTCOME:

The court may rule that SON is emancipated because he joined the military and, therefore, FATHER is no longer obligated to pay child support payments to MOTHER. However, if SON is discharged at the age or twenty after serving two years in the military, and returns to live with MOTHER, FATHER may once again be obligated to pay child support payments to MOTHER until SON reaches the age of 21.

# CHAPTER 6:
# CHILD ABUSE AND NEGLECT

**IN GENERAL**

The abuse or neglect of a child by one or both parents is a major factor considered by the court in awarding custody and granting visitation rights. For example, if it is demonstrated that the custodial parent has abused their child, depending on the type and extent of such abuse, custody may be transferred to the non-custodial parent. In addition, in more serious cases of abuse, a petition may be brought to have the offender's parental rights terminated. In addition, if a non-custodial parent has abused their child, efforts may be made to have visitation supervised.

**TYPES OF ABUSE**

Abuse takes many forms. As set forth in The Child Abuse Prevention Treatment Act, child abuse and neglect involves ". . .[t]he physical or mental injury (sexual abuse or exploitation, negligent treatment or maltreatment) of a child (a person under the age of 18, unless the child protection law of that state in which the child resides specifies a younger age for cases not involving sexual abuse) by a person (including any employee of a residential facility or any staff personnel providing out-of-home care) who is responsible for the child's welfare under circumstances which indicate that the child's health or welfare is harmed or threatened thereby. . ."

A discussion of the most common ways in which a child suffers abuse is set forth below.

### Physical Abuse

The Child Abuse Prevention Treatment Act defines physical abuse as "inflicting physical injury by punching, beating, kicking, biting, burning, or otherwise harming a child." Such injuries may have been unintentional and temporary, e.g. the injuries resulted from excessive physical punishment. Thus, corporal punishment that causes bruising or burning, and deprivations of food, water or needed medical treatment are all examples of physical abuse.

Studies have shown that parents who suffered abuse as children often repeat this behavior with their own children. Further, parents who suffer from drug or alcohol addiction are more likely to abuse their children. Abuse has also been found to exist to a greater degree when the home environment is under stress, e.g. a single-parent household, or a household suffering from depressed financial conditions, etc.

### Neglect

The Child Abuse Prevention Treatment Act defines child neglect as "the failure to provide the child's basic needs." This would include physical, educational or emotional needs. This would include, for example, the failure to seek necessary health care for a sick child, or the failure to enroll a school-age child in an educational program. The factors that indicate the likelihood of physical abuse in a particular household are substantially the same for child neglect.

### Emotional Abuse

It is often the case that a child's emotional well-being is ignored even though the child appears to be in good physical condition. However, the reality is that emotional abuse of a child often carries much deeper and long-lasting scars than a physical beating. Some examples of emotional abuse which negatively impair a child's psychological health include:

1. constant verbal assault on the child;

2. rejection;

3. punishment involving close confinement; and

4. the threat of physical harm.

Emotional abuse may also include speech and conduct designed to deprive the child of dignity and self-esteem, such as humiliating the child in front of family or friends, isolating the child from other persons for long periods of time and habitually directing language or gestures at the child that are designed to punish rather than instruct.

Children who have suffered psychological mistreatment are often characterized by low self-esteem and aggressive or other socially inappropriate behavior. Studies have shown that parents who suffered emotional neglect as children often repeat this behavior with their own children. Drug and alcohol addiction, a stressful home environment and the mental state of the parent are also known to contribute to this problem.

### Sexual Abuse

Child sexual abuse has been defined by the U.S. Department of Health and Human Services to include "fondling a child's genitals, intercourse, incest, rape, sodomy, exhibitionism and the sexual exploitation of a child." In general, sexual abuse includes virtually all behavior toward the child that is designed to lead to sexual gratification of either the adult or the child. While the most common forms of sexual abuse are those outright sexual acts described above, sexual abuse may also consist of placing the child in compromising situations such as nudity, inappropriate clothing, and imposing methods of discipline that are commonly associated with sexual gratification.

The child victims of sexual exploitation and sexual abuse, in general, come from a wide variety of family backgrounds, including all socio-economic classes and religions. Child victims of sexual abuse range in age from infancy through adolescence. Young children are often victimized by someone they know, e.g. a neighbor or family member. Many crave adult affection, and are lured into the behavior in an effort to obtain approval by adult authority figures.

The long-term effects on children who have been victims of sexual abuse are devastating. They are generally unable to form normal sexual relationships with persons of the opposite sex. Many child victims fall into destructive lifestyles, such as drug and alcohol addiction, and many succumb to suicide.

### Child Pornography and Prostitution

It is almost incomprehensible that parents may be responsible for involving their young children in the child pornography industry for financial gain. Nevertheless, it is a daily occurrence.

Child pornography and prostitution are highly organized, multi-million dollar industries that operate in our society on a nationwide scale. Sadly, parents often serve as perpetrators of this crime against their own children. In 1977, Congressional hearings were held on the subject of child pornography, also known as "kiddie porn." Witnesses who appeared before Congress told nightmare tales about small children who were kidnapped by pornographers, or sold to pornographers by their parents.

Outraged federal and state legislators have since attempted to enact laws to combat this widespread problem. Following the 1977 Congressional hearings, two federal statutes were passed: The Protection of

Children from Sexual Exploitation Act of 1977 and The Child Protection Act of 1984.

### The Protection of Children from Sexual Exploitation Act of 1977

The Protection of Children from Sexual Exploitation Act of 1977 prohibits the production of any sexually explicit material using a child under the age of sixteen, if such material is destined for, or has already traveled in interstate commerce.

In response to allegations that children were being sold by their parents into the pornography industry, the law was made applicable to parents or other custodians who knowingly permit a child to participate in the production of sexually explicit material.

### The Child Protection Act of 1984

Greater enforcement was subsequently obtained by enacting The Child Protection Act of 1984 which eliminated the requirement that child pornography distribution be undertaken for the purpose of "sale," and raised the age of protection to eighteen. In addition, penalties under the 1984 Act were greatly increased over those set forth in the 1977 Act, and a provision for criminal and civil forfeiture was included.

### STATE INTERVENTION

When both parents are guilty of abuse and/or neglect, the state—in its role as "*parens patriae*"—may step in and take custody of the child. This also occurs when a child is abandoned or orphaned. When the state intervenes in such situations, attempts are generally made to place the child with relatives.

A sample Child Protection Petition Alleging Child Abuse is set forth at Appendix 19.

A Sample Child Protection Petition Alleging Child Neglect is set forth at Appendix 20.

In the case of the death of a surviving parent, the will of the deceased may appoint a person to take custody of their minor child. If there are no relatives or appointees willing or available to take custody of the child, the state will provide living arrangements for the child. The child may be placed in a private foster home or a group home, many of which are owned and operated by the private sector or religious organizations. Efforts may also be made to place a child—particularly a younger child or infant—for adoption.

## FALSE ALLEGATIONS OF CHILD ABUSE

Allegations of some type of child abuse by one parent against the other often accompany modern-day child custody litigation. Such allegations may involve physical, emotional or sexual abuse. Unfortunately, some parents use the immoral tactic of making false allegations to gain an advantage in custody litigation.

Of course, the mere allegation of child abuse is disturbing and, once made, is difficult to retract. This is particularly destructive when the false allegation is one of sexual abuse. When such an allegation is made, the accused parent is usually deprived of contact with the child until a full investigation is conducted. Meanwhile, the child is subjected to a series of tests exploring sexual issues, and the accused parent is unfairly embarrassed by having to defend against such an allegation.

To make matters worse, there have been a number of instances where testing results in a contradictory result, or a false positive indication of sexual abuse. It is certainly known to be a difficult determination to make. Nevertheless, because a child who has been subjected to abuse—physical, emotional or sexual—must be protected at all costs, the mere allegation must be thoroughly explored and either confirmed or ruled out. This is so whether the abuser is a parent, another family member or a stranger.

# CHAPTER 7:
# ESTABLISHING PATERNITY

## IN GENERAL

Paternity refers to the relationship of a father to a child. In general, a father's parental rights are based on marriage to the mother or the establishment of paternity. In a marital relationship, there is a presumption that the husband is the father of any children born during the marriage. This presumption of paternity is not available to an unmarried father whereas the mother is always presumed to be the parent of her child.

## THE FATHER'S PARENTAL RIGHTS

Biological fathers who have demonstrated a commitment to the responsibilities of parenthood do have an interest in their child; however, this does not guarantee parental rights. The father's parental rights must be legally established in order for him to have the same rights regarding the child as the mother.

If the mother and father are married when the child is born, the father's parental rights are clearly established. If the mother then seeks to relinquish her rights to the child, the father does not lose his parental rights and can contest any action the mother takes concerning custody of the child, e.g. adoption. As long as the father is able to care for the child, he will maintain his parental rights.

For a number of reasons, it is important that the unmarried couple establish paternity of their biological children. For example, if the biological mother dies, the biological father, having established paternity, will not have to be concerned with any legal challenges to his right to custody of his biological children. In addition, if the unmarried couple separates, paternity must be established to obtain child support, custody, visitation, etc.

## FILING A PATERNITY PETITION

The father can establish paternity by filing a petition with the Family Court. A father may seek to establish paternity in order to obtain custody or visitation if the mother will not acknowledge his relationship to the child. Once the father establishes paternity, he will have the same rights and responsibilities towards the child as the mother. In addition, the mother will not have to take any further action to establish paternity, a prerequisite to obtaining child support.

If the father does not voluntarily admit to paternity, the mother must file a paternity petition and ask the court to make a determination as to paternity in order to obtain child support. Evidence, such as blood and DNA tests, will be produced to support the paternity petition. In addition to the child's mother and the man who is purportedly the child's father, a paternity suit may also be filed by the child, the child's guardian, and the Department of Social Services if the child is receiving public assistance.

Once paternity is established, the court will issue an order establishing paternity. The child is then legally entitled to the same rights and privileges as a child born of married parents, including the right to support, inheritance, and other benefits. In addition, the court can then rule on custody, visitation, and child support issues.

The paternity petition is generally filed in the state's Family Court. The person who starts the case is called the "petitioner." In most cases, the petitioner is one of the parents. The parent against whom the petition is brought is called the "respondent."

A Sample Paternity Petition is set forth at Appendix 21.

The petitioner and respondent are required to appear in court for a hearing on the date set forth in the court papers. At the hearing, provided they are in agreement, the child's mother and the alleged father testify that he is, in fact, the child's father, if that is the truth. The court will then sign an Order of Filiation naming the man as the child's legal father.

If the alleged father contests paternity, the court will order DNA tests on the mother, the alleged father and child for more evidence. By reviewing the DNA results, the court can decide whether the man named in the court papers is actually the child's father.

A sample Order of Filiation and Support is set forth at Appendix 22.

## PATERNITY TESTING

Paternity testing generally refers to the use of certain tests to match up DNA or specific blood proteins to determine whether a man is the father of a child. Paternity tests may be administered either before the child is born—i.e., prenatal testing—or after the child is born—i.e., postnatal testing.

### Prenatal DNA Tests

Prenatal DNA tests include the following:

#### Amniocentesis

Amniocentesis is performed in the second trimester, anywhere from the 14th-24th weeks of pregnancy. During this procedure, the doctor uses ultrasound to guide a thin needle into the mother's uterus, through the abdomen. The needle draws out a small amount of amniotic fluid, which is tested. Risks include a small chance of harming the baby and miscarriage. Other side effects may include cramping, leaking amniotic fluid, and vaginal bleeding. A doctor's consent is needed to do this procedure for paternity testing.

#### Chorionic Villus Sampling (CVS)

Chorionic Villus Sampling (CVS) consists of a thin needle or tube which a doctor inserts from the vagina, through the cervix, guided by an ultrasound, to obtain chorionic villi. Chorionic villi are little finger-like pieces of tissue attached to the wall of the uterus. The chorionic villi and the fetus come from the same fertilized egg, and have the same genetic makeup. This testing can be done earlier in pregnancy between the 10th-13th weeks. A doctor's consent is needed to do this procedure for paternity testing.

### Postnatal DNA Tests

Postnatal DNA tests include the following:

1. blood collection and testing;

2. cheek swab collection and testing;

3. umbilical cord collection and testing; and

4. other sample collection and testing, e.g., semen, tissue, hair, etc.

Paternity testing typically costs between $250.00 and $2,000.00, depending on the area in which you live in and the type of paternity test you choose. Prenatal testing is more costly that testing done after a baby is born. DNA testing results are usually available in 14 business days or less. Many DNA testing centers offer court-approved tests, however, it is advisable to check with the court to make sure the testing center is approved by the court.

## NAMING THE CHILD

In a marital relationship, the child usually takes the last name of the father and that is the name that appears on the child's birth certificate. Unmarried couples generally keep their own last names, thus, the question arises as to what last name should appear on the child's birth certificate as his or her legal name.

There is generally no requirement that the child of a married or unmarried couple take the last name of either parent. Thus, the child can have an entirely different last name if the parents so choose. However, this is rarely the case. Unmarried parents can use either the last name of the father or the mother, or they can choose to hyphenate both last names. If in the future the parents wish to amend the birth certificate—e.g., if they marry and want the child to use the father's last name—they can contact their state's bureau of vital statistics to amend the child's birth certificate.

The parents do not have to be married in order to have both names listed on the child's birth certificate, however, placing the father's name on the birth certificate does not in and of itself establish paternity. Most states require the father to sign an Acknowledgement of Paternity in order to be listed.

An Acknowledgment of Paternity is a form, usually filled out at the hospital at the time of a child's birth, on which the mother and father state that the man signing the paper is the father of the child. An Acknowledgment of Paternity does the same thing as a court Order of Filiation and will permit a hospital or Department of Health to name the man as the child's father on the birth certificate. Nevertheless, if the father's name was not listed at birth, the birth certificate can be amended as set forth above.

## CHILD'S ELIGIBILITY FOR GOVERNMENT BENEFITS

The children of an unmarried couple are eligible for government benefits, such as social security survivorship benefits should a parent become disabled or pass away. This is another reason paternity should be established as soon after birth as possible. For example, if the child's father passes away unexpectedly without having established paternity, and the father's name is not on the child's birth certificate, the child may be denied survivorship benefits due to lack of proof of parentage.

# CHAPTER 8:
# REPRODUCTIVE TECHNOLOGY AND CUSTODY

## IN GENERAL

Many couples who were previously unable to conceive have been given a new chance of having a child through recent innovations in reproductive technology. Sperm, embryos and ova can all now be frozen and thawed, without risk of damage, for later use by infertile couples.

As promising as these advances are, they have opened the door for new legal problems and ethical dilemmas. The courts are being bombarded by lawsuits arising from high-tech reproduction—the ability to unite sperm and egg in nontraditional ways. The issues these lawsuits raise show how slow the law has been to catch up with the technological changes.

## WHAT IS AN EMBRYO?

The term "embryo" refers to the early stages of development that occurs after a woman's egg is fertilized by a man's sperm. During weeks one through four following conception, the embryo plants itself to the mother's uterus. At this time, the umbilical cord and connections between the mother and embryo begin to form.

During weeks five through eight, the embryo produces chemicals that stop the mother's menstrual cycle. At this time, the brain begins to develop and the heart begins to beat. All the main organs are developed and growing, or beginning to develop. There are stubs visible where the arms and legs will later grow. The embryo's blood type can be discerned, and the eyes begin to form. In addition, the embryo is now capable of motion. It is at this more advanced stage of development—i.e., the eighth week of gestation—that the fetal stage begins and continues up until birth.

## FREEZING EMBRYOS

Freezing embryos—also known as cryopreservation—is now standard practice at in vitro fertilization (IVF) clinics because it is safer and more efficient than standard IVF treatment. Standard IVF treatment involves retrieving multiple eggs from a woman's ovaries, fertilizing those eggs and implanting them in the uterus at one time. However, many more eggs are retrieved than can be used during this process.

Freezing embryos allows for the fertilization of all of the retrieved eggs, implanting some of them in the uterus, and freezing the rest of the embryos for future use, if necessary or desired. It is estimated that there are presently approximately 150,000 frozen embryos.

## FROZEN EMBRYO LITIGATION

In most cases, cryopreservation of the embryos does not present any problem, however, in some cases, disputes over ownership of the frozen embryos has led to litigation. Cases are pending that ask the Court to determine custody rights of "potential" children.

This type of litigation is so new that there is no uniformity in the decisions rendered by the courts of various states. However, some legal experts believe a consensus on several related issues has begun to emerge. First, embryos should be categorized as a "special entity" with potential for life, and not children or property. In addition, most agree that an embryo disposition agreement should be considered a contract and enforced.

Frozen embryo lawsuits involve a number of different types of claims. Most disputes involve ownership of the frozen embryos following divorce. In one case, the husband wanted ownership of the frozen embryos in order to have them implanted in the uterus of a surrogate mother, and have the resulting children placed for adoption outside of the state. The wife in that case wanted ownership of the frozen embryos in case she wanted to have children in the future. The woman who supplied the eggs sided with the mother. The Washington court ruled for the husband.

In a case based on similar facts, a Michigan court ruled in favor of the husband, stating that the husband had a right to choose not to have more children. In a similar Illinois case, the husband did not want his wife to become pregnant with any more of his children following the divorce. The court ruled that custody of the embryos would be decided as part of the divorce trial.

In addition, two state courts—New York and New Jersey— have ruled that the frozen embryos can be destroyed even if one of the parents wants a chance to give them life. Neither of the judges considered the humanity of the frozen embryos, but based the decision solely on contract law.

In a case that sought to refine the definition of motherhood, a Court denied the request of a surrogate mother for parental rights to the child she bore for another couple, saying she had served in the transitory role of a foster parent. Declaring that two parents are better than three, the judge terminated the visitation rights of the surrogate mother, and ruled that the child is to remain in the custody of his or her genetic parents.

## OHIO HOUSE BILL 102–126TH GENERAL ASSEMBLY

Ohio has tried to deal with the issues arising from frozen embryo litigation. In 2005, they introduced legislation intended to address an ambiguous situation involving custody of frozen embryos—i.e., which "mother" would be considered the child's legal mother in a contested custody dispute in which a donated embryo was gestated and birthed by a woman who intends to raise the child as her own. In addition, there is no controlling law addressing how the intended father is to be treated legally. The proposed law attempts to clarify the parentage of certain children born as a result of embryo donation.

Under the bill, a woman who gives birth to a child born as a result of embryo donation is the natural mother of the resulting child, and the child is the natural child of that woman. Filing a parentage action cannot change the woman's status as the child's mother, and the genetic mother of the child is therefore eliminated as a potential legal mother. The bill does not deal with surrogacy contracts, because it applies only to embryo donation for the purpose of impregnating a woman so that she can bear a child that she intends to raise as her own.

Further, the Act provides that if a woman who gives birth to a child through embryo donation is married, and her husband consents to the embryo donation, the husband is the natural father of the child. A presumption of a father and child relation that arises from the man being married to the woman is conclusive with respect to this father and child relationship, and no action or proceeding under the parentage law can affect the relationship.

The bill does not address the paternity of children born as a result of embryo donation when the intended parents are not married. Unless the intended father files an acknowledgment of paternity or adopts the child, it does not appear that he would automatically be considered the child's legal father in the event of a custody dispute.

## EMBRYO DISPOSITION AGREEMENT

Prior to opting for embryonic cryopreservation, couples are advised to discuss the legal implications of doing so with their lawyer. They may want to enter into an embryo disposition agreement that sets forth who will have custody of the embryos if the couple decides to split up, or whether the embryos should be destroyed.

It has been suggested that legislation should be enacted which would require and protect the enforceability of an embryo disposition agreement. Such an agreement would help prevent litigation in this area.

# APPENDIX 1:
# CHILD CUSTODY CRITERIA

| STATE | FACTORS CONSIDERED |
|---|---|
| Alabama | Statutory guidelines; children's wishes; joint custody; domestic violence |
| Alaska | Statutory guidelines; children's wishes; joint custody; cooperative parent; domestic violence; health |
| Arizona | Statutory guidelines; children's wishes; joint custody; cooperative parent; domestic violence; health |
| Arkansas | Domestic violence |
| California | Statutory guidelines; children's wishes; cooperative parent; domestic violence; health |
| Colorado | Statutory guidelines; children's wishes; cooperative parent; joint custody; domestic violence; health |
| Connecticut | Children's wishes; joint custody |
| Delaware | Statutory guidelines; children's wishes; health |
| District of Columbia | Statutory guidelines; children's wishes; joint custody; cooperative parent; domestic violence; health |
| Florida | Statutory guidelines; children's wishes; joint custody; cooperative parent; domestic violence; health |
| Georgia | Statutory guidelines; children's wishes; joint custody; domestic violence |
| Hawaii | Statutory guidelines; children's wishes; joint custody; domestic violence |
| Idaho | Statutory guidelines; children's wishes; joint custody; domestic violence; health |
| Illinois | Statutory guidelines; children's wishes; joint custody; cooperative parent; domestic violence; health |
| Indiana | Statutory guidelines; children's wishes; joint custody; cooperative parent; domestic violence; health |
| Iowa | Statutory guidelines; children's wishes; joint custody; cooperative parent; domestic violence; health |

| STATE | FACTORS CONSIDERED |
|---|---|
| Kansas | Statutory guidelines; children's wishes; joint custody; cooperative parent; domestic violence; health |
| Kentucky | Statutory guidelines; children's wishes; joint custody; cooperative parent; domestic violence; health |
| Louisiana | Statutory guidelines; children's wishes; joint custody; domestic violence |
| Maine | Statutory guidelines; children's wishes; joint custody; domestic violence |
| Maryland | Children's wishes; joint custody; cooperative parent; domestic violence; health |
| Massachusetts | Joint custody; domestic violence |
| Michigan | Statutory guidelines; children's wishes; joint custody; cooperative parent; domestic violence; health |
| Minnesota | Statutory guidelines; children's wishes; joint custody; domestic violence; health |
| Mississippi | Statutory guidelines; joint custody; health |
| Missouri | Statutory guidelines; children's wishes; joint custody; cooperative parent; domestic violence; health |
| Montana | Statutory guidelines; children's wishes; joint custody; domestic violence |
| Nebraska | Statutory guidelines; children's wishes; joint custody; domestic violence; health |
| Nevada | Statutory guidelines; children's wishes; joint custody; cooperative parent; domestic violence |
| New Hampshire | Statutory guidelines; children's wishes; joint custody; domestic violence |
| New Jersey | Statutory guidelines; children's wishes; joint custody; cooperative parent; domestic violence; health |
| New Mexico | Statutory guidelines; children's wishes; joint custody; cooperative parent; domestic violence; health |
| New York | Children's wishes; domestic violence |
| North Carolina | Children's wishes; joint custody; domestic violence; health |
| North Dakota | Statutory guidelines; children's wishes; joint custody; cooperative parent; domestic violence; health |
| Ohio | Statutory guidelines; children's wishes; joint custody; domestic violence; health |
| Oklahoma | Statutory guidelines; children's wishes; joint custody; cooperative parent; domestic violence |
| Oregon | Statutory guidelines; children's wishes; joint custody; cooperative parent; domestic violence |

| STATE | FACTORS CONSIDERED |
|---|---|
| Pennsylvania | Statutory guidelines; children's wishes; joint custody; co-operative parent; domestic violence; health |
| Rhode Island | Children's wishes; joint custody; cooperative parent; domestic violence; health |
| South Carolina | Children's wishes; joint custody; cooperative parent; domestic violence; health |
| South Dakota | Children's wishes; joint custody; cooperative parent; domestic violence |
| Tennessee | Statutory guidelines; children's wishes; joint custody; co-operative parent; domestic violence |
| Texas | Statutory guidelines; children's wishes; joint custody; co-operative parent; domestic violence; health |
| Utah | Statutory guidelines; children's wishes; joint custody; co-operative parent |
| Vermont | Statutory guidelines; joint custody; domestic violence |
| Virginia | Statutory guidelines; children's wishes; joint custody; co-operative parent; domestic violence; health |
| Washington | Statutory guidelines; children's wishes; domestic violence; health |
| West Virginia | Children's wishes; joint custody; domestic violence |
| Wisconsin | Statutory guidelines; children's wishes; joint custody; co-operative parent; domestic violence; health |
| Wyoming | Children's wishes; joint custody; domestic violence |

Source: American Bar Association, Family Law Section.

# APPENDIX 2:
# CLAUSE CONCERNING RELIGIOUS
# UPBRINGING

The parties agree that, in order to maintain the continuity of the child's [name of religious affiliation] religious affiliation and education, the child will be brought up in the Catholic and will continue to attend [School Name and Address], or in the event that the child shall relocate out of the district/parish of said school, the child will attend [name of religious affiliation] of the district/parish which serves the child's new home.

# APPENDIX 3:
# JOINT CUSTODY AGREEMENT

THIS AGREEMENT, made this [Insert Date of Agreement], by and between [Name and Address of Father] (hereinafter referred to as "Father") and [Name and Address of Mother] (hereinafter referred to as "Mother"),

WITNESSETH:

WHEREAS, the parties were divorced on the [Insert Date of Divorce], in the [City/County/State]; and

WHEREAS, there is one child born of the marriage, to wit [Name/Age/Date of Birth of Child] (hereinafter referred to as the "child"); and

WHEREAS, the parties desire to resolve the custody arrangements of their minor child;

NOW THEREFORE, in consideration of the promises and undertakings herein set forth both parties do hereby covenant and agree as follows:

1. Father and Mother shall have joint legal custody of their minor child and equal input into all matters relating to the child's health, education and welfare.

2. Father is hereby designated as primary residential custodian of the child.

3. Father shall not relocate the child from the [Name of State]. If Father desires to relocate outside of the [Name of State], Mother shall become the primary residential custodian of the child.

4. Father and Mother agree to share physical custody of the child according to the following schedule:

(a) Every Wednesday throughout the year, except as may conflict with the holiday schedule as set forth in (c) below, the child shall be in the physical custody of the Mother, who will retrieve the child at 5:30 p.m. from the custodial residence, and return the child the following morning at 8:00 a.m., for the child's timely delivery by the Mother to school, or on non-school days, to the custodial residence.

(b) Every other weekend throughout the year, except as may conflict with the holiday schedule as set forth in (c) below, the child shall be in the physical custody of the Mother, who will retrieve the child at 5:30 p.m. on Friday from the custodial residence, and return the child at 8:00 a.m. on Monday morning, for the child's timely delivery by Mother to school, or on non-school days, to the custodial residence.

(c) The following holiday schedule shall take precedence over the above regular schedule:

(i) On holidays which fall on a Monday, the child shall remain with the parent who has had the child for that weekend. If the child is in the physical custody of the Mother, the Mother shall return the child at 8:00 a.m. on Tuesday morning, for the child's timely delivery by Mother to school, or on non-school days, to the custodial residence.

(ii) Effective as of the date of this Agreement, the child shall spend alternating Thanksgiving Holidays with the Mother in odd-numbered years and the Father in even-numbered years.

(iii) Effective as of the date of this Agreement, the child shall spend alternating Easter Holidays with the Mother in even-numbered years and the Father in odd-numbered years.

(iv) Effective as of the date of this Agreement, the child shall spend alternating Christmas Eve Holidays with the Mother in odd-numbered years and the Father in even-numbered years, beginning at 3:00 p.m. on December 24th through 10:00 a.m. on December 25th.

(v) Effective as of the date of this Agreement, the child shall spend alternating Christmas Day Holidays with the Mother in even-numbered years and the Father in odd-numbered years, beginning at 10:00 a.m. on December 25th through December 26th at 10:00 a.m.

(d) The parties agree to the following vacation schedule:

(i) Each party is entitled to physical custody of the child for one-half of the summer vacation, with the dates to be established no later than May 31st.

(ii) Each party is entitled to physical custody of the child for one-half of the designated spring recess, with the dates and times to be agreed upon between the parties.

(iii) Each party is entitled to physical custody of the child for one-half of the designated winter recess, with the dates and times to be agreed upon between the parties.

5. The parties may, upon mutual agreement, amend the above schedule to accommodate the demands of work, illness, school schedules, or for other good cause.

IN WITNESS WHEREOF, the parties have signed, sealed and acknowledged this Agreement as of the date first written above.

_____

SIGNATURE LINE–FATHER


_____

SIGNATURE LINE–MOTHER


NOTARY STAMP

# APPENDIX 4:
# CO-PARENTING AGREEMENT

## CO-PARENTING AGREEMENT

This agreement is made this _____ day of _____, 20__, by and between [name of legal parent] and [name of non-legal parent], hereafter referred to as the "parties."

This agreement as made is prepared to set out our rights and obligations regarding [name of child], t.he biological/legal child of [name of legal parent] and non-legal child of [name of non-legal parent] (hereinafter referred to as "the child"). We realize state law, as far as a child is concerned, limits our power to contract. We also understand that the law will recognize [name of legal mother/father] as the only mother/father of the child.

In the spirit of cooperation and mutual respect, we state the following terms as our agreement:

1. Each clause of this agreement is separate and divisible from the others. Should a court refuse to enforce one or more clauses of this agreement, the others are still valid and in full force.

2. Our intention is to jointly and equally share parental responsibility, with both of us providing support and guidance to the child. We will make every effort to jointly share the responsibilities of raising the child, including but not limited to providing food, clothing and shelter, educating and making medical decisions.

3. Consent for medical authorization will be signed by [name of legal parent] giving [name of non-legal parent] equal power to make medical decisions she/he thinks are necessary for the child.

4. The parties will each pay one-half of the out-of-pocket costs to provide the child with food, shelter, child care, clothing, medical and dental care, counseling and any medical or educational expenses necessary to promote her/his welfare.

5. The child will have the last name [child's last name]. The child's first and middle name(s) will be determined by mutual consent.

6. [Name of legal parent] agrees to designate [name of non-legal parent] as guardian of the child in her/his will. We understand that naming [name of non-legal parent] as legal guardian of the child in [name of legal parent's] will is not legally binding. However, parties wish to express their clear intentions that this agreement should be submitted to any court that is reviewing these matters.

7. The parties acknowledge and agree that they will make all major decisions regarding physical location, support, education and medical care of the child.

8. Prior to any separation between the parties, the parties agree to participate in a jointly agreed-upon program of counseling if either of us considers separating from the other.

9. In the event of a separation between the parties, each party will do his/her best to see that the child grows up in a good and healthy environment. Specifically, the parties agree that:

(a) We will do our best to make sure that the child maintains a close and loving relationship with both of us.

(b) We will share in the child's upbringing and will share in the child's support, depending on our needs, the child's needs and on our respective abilities to pay.

(c) We will make a good-faith effort to jointly make all major decisions affecting the child's health and welfare, and all decisions will be based upon the best interests of the child.

(d) Should the child spend a greater portion of the year living with one of us, the person who has actual physical custody will take all steps necessary to maximize the other's visitation and help make visitation as easy as possible.

(e) If either of us dies, the child will be cared for and raised by the other, whether or not we are living together. We will each state this in our wills.

10. Should any dispute arise between us regarding this agreement, we agree to submit the dispute first to mediation. If mediation is not successful, we agree to submit to binding arbitration, sharing the cost equally.

11. We agree that if any court finds any portion of this contract illegal or otherwise unenforceable, the rest of the contract is still valid and in full force.

_____

SIGNATURE LINE—LEGAL PARENT


_____

SIGNATURE LINE—NON-LEGAL PARENT

# APPENDIX 5:
## STATE CUSTODY CASES INVOLVING SAME-SEX PARTNERS

| STATE | CASE CITATION | COURT DECISION |
|---|---|---|
| CALIFORNIA | Curiale v. Reagan, 222 Cal. App.3d 1597 (1990) | The Court of Appeals held that a non-biological parent did not have standing to bring an action to establish the existence of a parent-child relationship. The court opined that the California legislature had not given non-parent same-sex partners any right of custody or visitation upon termination of the relationship. |
| CALIFORNIA | Nancy S. v. Michele G., 228 Cal. App. 3d 831 (1991) | The Court of Appeals held that even if the non-biological mother could establish that she was a "de facto" parent, she would not be able to seek custody or visitation over the objections of the legal mother. A "de facto" parent can only be awarded custody if it is shown by clear and convincing evidence that parental custody is detrimental to the children. |

| STATE | CASE CITATION | COURT DECISION |
|---|---|---|
| CALIFORNIA | West v. Superior Court, 59 Cal. App. 4th 302 (1997) | The Court of Appeals held that the trial court did not have subject matter jurisdiction to enter an order granting visitation to a former same-sex partner. The court declined to confer standing to the non-biological mother who did not adopt the child. |
| CALIFORNIA | Elisa B. v. Superior Court, K.M. v. E.G., Kristine H. v. Lisa R. (CA 2005) | In three separate decisions, the California Supreme Court held that when a couple deliberately brings a child into the world through the use of assisted reproduction, both partners are legal parents, regardless of their gender or marital status, and that children born to same-sex couples must be treated equally to other children and thus have a legally protected relationship to both partners. |
| COLORADO | In the Interest of E.L.M.C., 2004 WL 1469410 (Colo. Ct. App. 2004) | The Court of Appeals held that a non-adoptive parent had standing to petition for equal parenting time because she had become the child's psychological parent and there was a risk of emotional harm to the child if visitation were to be terminated. The court upheld a Colorado statute that allows non-parents who have had a recent or continuing role as a caretaker to petition for parenting responsibilities. |
| CONNECTICUT | Music v. Rachford, 654 So. 2d 1234 (Fla. Ct. App. 1995) | Court of Appeals rejected the non-biological mother's claim that she was a "de facto" parent and entitled to shared parental responsibilities and visitation. |

| STATE | CASE CITATION | COURT DECISION |
|-------|---------------|----------------|
| CONNECTICUT | Laspina-Williams v. Laspina-Williams, 742 A.2d 840 (Conn. Super. 1999) | The court held that a non-biological mother had standing under a Connecticut law, which allows anyone to petition for visitation. The statute does not define the relationship necessary to give standing. The court opined that the bio-logical mother allowed, even encouraged, the plaintiff to assume a significant role in the life of the child such that she was entitled to seek visitation. |
| FLORIDA | Meeks v. Garner, 598 So. 2d 261 (Fla. Ct. App. 1992) | Court of Appeals held that visitation rights are purely stat-utory and that the former partner of the biological mother did not have a statutory right to seek visitation. |
| FLORIDA | Von Eiff v. Azicri, 720 So. 2d 510 (Fla. 1998) | Supreme Court reaffirmed adoptive or biological parents' rights to make decisions about their children's welfare without interference by third parties. |
| FLORIDA | Kazmierazak v. Query, 736 So.2d 106 (Fla. Ct. App. 1999) | The Court of Appeals held that a psychological parent is not entitled to the equivalent parental status as the biolog-ical parent. The court acknowledged that it had recognized the concept of "psychological parent" in the past, but opined that it could not construe previous "psychological parent" cases as giving equal parental status to non-bio-logical or non-adoptive parents. The court further held that the concept of "in loco parentis" is only applicable to cases that arise within the context of a marital relationship. |
| ILLINOIS | In re C.B.L., 723 N.E.2d 316 (Ill. Ct. App. 1999) | The Court of Appeals held that the non-biological mother did not have standing as a common law "de facto" parent or as an individual "in loco parentis" to the child that she helped raise with her former partner because the Marriage Act had been revised so many times that it superseded and supplanted the common law. |

| STATE | CASE CITATION | COURT DECISION |
|---|---|---|
| INDIANA | In re A.B., 818 N.E.2d 126 (Ind. Ct. App. 2004) | The Court of Appeals held that as a matter of law, "when two women involved in a domestic relationship agree to bear and raise a child together by artificial insemination of one of the partners with semen from a donor, both women are the legal parents of the resulting child," without the need for an adoption. |
| MAINE | C.E.W. v. D.E.W., 845 A.2d 1146 (ME 2004) | Court held that the non-biological mother was a de facto parent of a child that she helped raise with her former partner making her eligible to be considered for disbursement of parental rights and responsibilities. |
| MARYLAND | S.F. v. M.D., 751 A.2d 9 (Md. 2000) | Court held that it was within its discretion when it used the "best interest" standard to deny the petition of a non-biological mother who sought visitation as a de facto parent. |
| MASSACHUSETTS | E.N.O. v. L.M.M., 711 N.E.2d 886 (Mass. 1999) | The Court held that it had equitable jurisdiction to award visitation to the biological mother's former same-sex partner. The court determined that the non-biological mother was a de facto parent because she had participated in the child's life as a member of the family, lived with the child, and, with the consent and encouragement of the legal parent, performed a share of the caretaking functions at least as great as the legal parent. |
| MICHIGAN | McGuffin v. Overton, 542 N.W. 2d 288 (Mich. Ct. App. 1995) | Court of Appeals denied same-sex partner's petition for custody of deceased biological mother's children, despite wishes expressed in will, when biological father assumed physical custody of children. Court held that she lacked standing to file for custody because she did not meet the statutory requirement of being related to the children "within the fifth degree by marriage, blood, or adoption." |

| STATE | CASE CITATION | COURT DECISION |
|-------|---------------|----------------|
| MINNESOTA | LaChappelle v. Mitten, 607 N.W. 2d 151 (Minn. Ct. App. 2000) | Court of Appeals permitted a non-biological mother to seek custody under a statute that allows people other than parents to seek custody under certain circumstances. The court reasoned that by agreeing to share custody of the child with the non-biological mother, the biological mother had functionally abandoned her right to sole legal custody and that that joint legal custody was in the child's best interest. |
| MISSOURI | Matter of T.L., 1996 WL 393521 (Mo.Cir.1996) | In a petition for custody, the court treated the non-biological mother as an "equitable parent" because she provided for the physical, emotional, and social needs of a child, and demonstrated that (1) she had physical custody of the child for an extended period; (2) her motive in seeking parental status was her genuine care and concern for the child; and (3) her relationship with the child began with the consent of the child's legal parent. It held that as an equitable parent, the non-biological mother could be awarded visitation with the child, absent a finding of parental unfitness, since the minor child's growth and development would be detrimentally affected by elimination of contact with the equitable parent. |
| NEW JERSEY | V.C. v. M.J.B., 748 A. 2d 539 (N.J 2000) | A non-biological mother was awarded visitation because she qualified as a psychological parent and had forged a parent-like relationship with the consent of the biological parent. |

| STATE | CASE CITATION | COURT DECISION |
|---|---|---|
| NEW MEXICO | A.C. v. C.B., 829 P.2d 660 (N.M. Ct. App. 1992) | Court of Appeals held that former same-sex partner had standing to visitation when the biological mother breached a settlement agreement regarding time-sharing and co-parenting. The court also held that sexual orientation, standing alone, is not a permissible basis for denial of custody or visitation rights. |
| NEW MEXICO | Barnae v. Barnae, 943 P.2d 1036 (N.M. Ct. App. 1997) | Court held that a same-sex partner who is not a biological parent has standing to assert a legal right to a continuing relationship with a child. |
| NEW YORK | Alison D. v. Virginia M., 569 N.Y.S.2d 586 (1991) | Court held that former same-sex partner of the biological mother, who attempted to seek visitation as a "de facto" parent or a parent "by estoppel", did not have standing to seek visitation over the objections of a fit legal parent where she did not meet the definition of a parent for the purposes of a New York statute that grants the right to seek visitation or change of custody to "either parent." |
| OHIO | Liston v. Pyles, 1997 WL 467327 (Ohio Ct. App. 1997) | Court of Appeals held that the former same-sex partner of the biological mother did not have standing to seek visitation because she failed to prove that she was related to the child by blood or marriage, and that she was not related by affinity because same-sex marriage is not recognized by Ohio. The Court also held that the doctrine of "in loco parentis" did not create a duty of support and/or a right to visitation under the facts of the case. |
| OHIO | In re Jones, 2002 WL 940195 (Ohio Ct. App. 2002) | Court of Appeals held that the biological mother who allowed the non-biological mother to be a part of the child's life had not relinquished custody and could terminate visitation between the child and the non-parent. |

| STATE | CASE CITATION | COURT DECISION |
|---|---|---|
| PENNSYLVANIA | T.B. v. L.R.M., 786 A.2d 913 (Pa. 2001) | Court held that a non-biological mother who assumed parental status and discharged parental duties with the consent of the biological parent had standing to seek visitation under the doctrine of in loco parentis |
| RHODE ISLAND | Rubano v. DiCenzo, 759 A.2d 959 (R.I. 2000) | Court held that the Family Court had jurisdiction to determine the existence of a de facto parental relationship between a same-sex parent and a child with whom she had no biological relationship, and to enforce the biological mother's settlement agreement allowing the non-biological parent to visit with the child. |
| TENNESSEE | In re Thompson, 11 S.W.3d 913 (Tenn. Ct. App. 1999) | Court of Appeals held that the Tennessee legislature had not given a right of custody or visitation to a non-parent who is not and has not been married to either of the children's parents, but who previously maintained an intimate relationship with such a parent and who previously provided care and support to the children. |
| TEXAS | Coons v. Anderson, 104 S.W.3d 630 (Tex. App. Ct. 2003) | Court of Appeals held that a person standing "in loco parentis" has a right to ask for visitation, but that non-biological mother whose visitation was cut off by biological mother was not "in loco parentis" at the relevant time because she filed the petition more than 90 days after her separation from the biological mother, and the statute requires that the parent seeking visitation has had actual care, custody, and possession of the child for not less than six months and ending not more than 90 days preceding the filing of the petition. |

| STATE | CASE CITATION | COURT DECISION |
|---|---|---|
| VERMONT | Titchenal v. Dexter, 693 A.2d 682 (Vt. 1997) | Court held that the state's "parens patriae" power does not give the superior court jurisdiction to hear disputes regarding parent-child relationships outside statutory proceedings, and plaintiff failed to show a statutory, common law, or constitutional basis for applying equitable jurisdiction in order to extend a right to parent-child contact to an "equitable" or "de facto" parent. |
| WASHINGTON | In re the Parentage of L.B., 89 P.3d 271 (Wash. Ct. App. 2004) | Court of Appeals held that a petition for shared parentage or visitation will only be entertained if the petitioner can prove that a parent-like relationship developed with the consent and encouragement of the biological parent, and that there was some triggering event, such as the legal parent's denial of visitation with the child. |
| WISCONSIN | In re H.S.H.-K., 533 N.W.2d 419 (Wis. 1995) | Court used its equitable jurisdiction to allow a non-biological parent to seek visitation where petitioner could prove that the legal parent consented to and fostered the formation of a parent-like relationship with the child, that petitioner lived with the child, that petitioner performed parental functions for the child to a significant degree, and that a parent-child bond was forged. |

SOURCE: National Center for Lesbian Rights (NCLR).

# APPENDIX 6:
# THIRD PARTY VISITATION RIGHTS

| STATE | PARTIES PERMITTED TO PETITION FOR THIRD PARTY VISITATION |
|---|---|
| Alabama | Grandparent in case of death of child; grandparent in case of divorce of child |
| Alaska | Stepparent; grandparent in case of death of child; grandparent in case of divorce of child; parent of child born out of wedlock; any interested party |
| Arizona | Stepparent; grandparent in case of death of child; grandparent in case of divorce of child; parent of child born out of wedlock; any interested party |
| Arkansas | Stepparent; grandparent in case of death of child; grandparent in case of divorce of child |
| California | Stepparent; grandparent in case of death of child; grandparent in case of divorce of child; any interested party |
| Colorado | Grandparent in case of death of child; grandparent in case of divorce of child; parent of child born out of wedlock |
| Connecticut | Stepparent; grandparent in case of death of child; grandparent in case of divorce of child; parent of child born out of wedlock; any interested party |
| Delaware | Stepparent; grandparent in case of divorce of child |
| District of Columbia | None listed |
| Florida | Grandparent in case of death of child; grandparent in case of divorce of child; parent of child born out of wedlock |
| Georgia | Grandparent in case of death of child; grandparent in case of divorce of child |
| Hawaii | Stepparent; grandparent in case of divorce of child |
| Idaho | Grandparent in case of divorce of child; parent of child born out of wedlock |

| STATE | PARTIES PERMITTED TO PETITION FOR THIRD PARTY VISITATION |
|---|---|
| Illinois | Stepparent; grandparent in case of death of child; grandparent in case of divorce of child; parent of child born out of wedlock |
| Indiana | Stepparent; grandparent in case of death of child; grandparent in case of divorce of child; parent of child born out of wedlock |
| Iowa | Grandparent in case of death of child; grandparent in case of divorce of child; parent of child born out of wedlock |
| Kansas | Stepparent; grandparent in case of death of child; grandparent in case of divorce of child; parent of child born out of wedlock |
| Kentucky | Grandparent in case of death of child; grandparent in case of divorce of child; parent of child born out of wedlock; any interested party |
| Louisiana | Stepparent under extraordinary circumstances; grandparent in case of death of child; grandparent in case of divorce of child |
| Maine | Stepparent; grandparent in case of death of child; grandparent in case of divorce of child; parent of child born out of wedlock |
| Maryland | Grandparent in case of death of child; grandparent in case of divorce of child |
| Massachusetts | Grandparent in case of death of child; grandparent in case of divorce of child; parent of child born out of wedlock |
| Michigan | Stepparent; grandparent in case of death of child; grandparent in case of divorce of child |
| Minnesota | Stepparent; grandparent in case of death of child; grandparent in case of divorce of child; parent of child born out of wedlock |
| Mississippi | Grandparent in case of death of child; grandparent in case of divorce of child |
| Missouri | Grandparent in case of death of child; grandparent in case of divorce of child; parent of child born out of wedlock |
| Montana | Grandparent in case of death of child; grandparent in case of divorce of child; parent of child born out of wedlock |
| Nebraska | Stepparent; grandparent in case of death of child; grandparent in case of divorce of child; parent of child born out of wedlock |

| STATE | PARTIES PERMITTED TO PETITION FOR THIRD PARTY VISITATION |
|---|---|
| Nevada | Grandparent in case of death of child; grandparent in case of divorce of child; parent of child born out of wedlock |
| New Hampshire | Stepparent; grandparent in case of death of child; grandparent in case of divorce of child; parent of child born out of wedlock |
| New Jersey | Stepparent; grandparent in case of death of child; grandparent in case of divorce of child; parent of child born out of wedlock |
| New Mexico | Stepparent; grandparent in case of death of child; grandparent in case of divorce of child; parent of child born out of wedlock; any interested party |
| New York | Stepparent; grandparent in case of death of child; grandparent in case of divorce of child; parent of child born out of wedlock |
| North Carolina | Grandparent in case of divorce of child |
| North Dakota | Stepparent; grandparent in case of death of child; grandparent in case of divorce of child; parent of child born out of wedlock |
| Ohio | Stepparent; grandparent in case of death of child; grandparent in case of divorce of child; parent of child born out of wedlock; interested third party provided they are related to minor child |
| Oklahoma | Grandparent in case of death of child; grandparent in case of divorce of child; parent of child born out of wedlock |
| Oregon | Stepparent; grandparent in case of death of child; grandparent in case of divorce of child; parent of child born out of wedlock; any interested party |
| Pennsylvania | Grandparent in case of death of child; grandparent in case of divorce of child |
| Rhode Island | Grandparent in case of death of child; grandparent in case of divorce of child |
| South Carolina | Grandparent in case of death of child; grandparent in case of divorce of child; parent of child born out of wedlock |
| South Dakota | Grandparent in case of death of child; grandparent in case of divorce of child; parent of child born out of wedlock |
| Tennessee | Stepparent; Grandparent in case of divorce of child |
| Texas | Stepparent; grandparent in case of death of child; grandparent in case of divorce of child; parent of child born out of wedlock; any interested party |

| STATE | PARTIES PERMITTED TO PETITION FOR THIRD PARTY VISITATION |
|---|---|
| Utah | Stepparent; grandparent in case of death of child; grandparent in case of divorce of child; parent of child born out of wedlock; any interested party |
| Vermont | Grandparent in case of death of child; grandparent in case of divorce of child |
| Virginia | Interested third party |
| Washington | Stepparent; grandparent in case of divorce of child |
| West Virginia | Grandparent in case of death of child; grandparent in case of divorce of child; parent of child born out of wedlock |
| Wisconsin | Grandparent in case of divorce of child |
| Wyoming | Stepparent; grandparent in case of death of child; grandparent in case of divorce of child; parent of child born out of wedlock; any interested party |

Source: American Bar Association, Family Law Section.

# APPENDIX 7:
# STATE STATUTES GOVERNING
# GRANDPARENT VISITATION

| STATE | STATUTE | GENERAL PROVISIONS |
|-------|---------|--------------------|
| Alabama | Alabama Code § 30-3-3 | Upon death of parent (child of grandparent) or during divorce, separation, annulment or child custody proceedings between parents. |
| Alaska | Alaska Statutes § 25.24.150 | Upon death of parent (child of grandparent) or during divorce, separation, annulment or child custody proceedings between parents. |
| Arizona | Arizona Revised Statutes Annotated § 25-337.01 | Upon death of parent (child of grandparent) or during divorce, separation, annulment or child custody proceedings between parents. |
| Arkansas | Arkansas Statutes Annotated § 9-13-103 | Upon death of parent (child of grandparent) or during divorce, separation, annulment or child custody proceedings between parents. |
| California | California Civil Code §§ 197.5; 4601 | Upon death of parent (child of grandparent) other circumstances under which grandparent visitation could be obtained are unspecified. |
| Colorado | Colorado Revised Statutes § 19-1-116 | Upon death of parent (child of grandparent) or during divorce, separation, annulment or child custody proceedings between parents. |

| STATE | STATUTE | GENERAL PROVISIONS |
|---|---|---|
| Connecticut | Connecticut General Statutes Annotated 6646b-59-59a | Circumstances under which grandparent visitation could be obtained are unspecified. |
| Delaware | Delaware Code Annotated, Title 10, § 950(7) | During divorce, separation, annulment or child custody proceedings between parents. |
| Florida | Florida Statutes § 61.13(2); (b)2c | During divorce, separation, annulment or child custody proceedings between parents. |
| Georgia | Georgia Code Annotated § 19-7-3 | Upon death of parent (child of grandparent). |
| Hawaii | Hawaii Revised Statutes § 571.46(7) | During divorce, separation, annulment or child custody proceedings between parents. |
| Idaho | Idaho Code § 32-1008 | Circumstances under which grandparent visitation could be obtained is unspecified. |
| Illinois | Illinois Annotated Statutes, Chapter 40, § 607(b)(c) | Upon death of parent (child of grandparent) or during divorce, separation, annulment or child custody proceedings between parents. |
| Indiana | Indiana Code Annotated §§ 31-1-11.7-1 to 7-8 | Upon death of parent (child of grandparent) or during divorce, separation, annulment or child custody proceedings between parents. |
| Iowa | Iowa Code Annotated §§ 598.35-36. | Upon death of parent (child of grandparent) or during divorce, separation, annulment or child custody proceedings between parents. |
| Kansas | Kansas Statutes Annotated § 60-1616(b) | Circumstances under which grandparent visitation could be obtained are unspecified. |
| Kentucky | Kentucky Revised Statutes Annotated § 405.021 | Circumstances under which grandparent visitation could be obtained are unspecified. |
| Louisiana | Louisiana Revised Statutes Annotated § 9:572 | Upon death of parent (child of grandparent) or during divorce, separation, annulment or child custody proceedings between parents. |

| STATE | STATUTE | GENERAL PROVISIONS |
|---|---|---|
| Maine | Maine Revised Statutes Annotated, Title 19 § 752 | Circumstances under which grandparent visitation could be obtained are unspecified. |
| Maryland | Maryland Family Law Code Annotated § 9-102 | During divorce, separation, annulment or child custody proceedings between parents. |
| Massachusetts | Massachusetts General Laws Annotated, Chapter 119 § 39D | Upon death of parent (child of grandparent) or during divorce, separation, annulment or child custody proceedings between parents. |
| Michigan | Michigan Compiled Laws Annotated § 722.72(b) | Upon death of parent (child of grandparent) or during divorce, separation, annulment or child custody proceedings between parents. |
| Minnesota | Minnesota Statutes Annotated § 257.022 | Upon death of parent (child of grandparent) or during divorce, separation, annulment or child custody proceedings between parents; or depending on the amount of time child lived with grandparent. |
| Mississippi | Mississippi Code Annotated §§ 93-16-1 | Upon death of parent (child of grandparent) or during divorce, separation, annulment or child custody proceedings between parents. |
| Missouri | Missouri Annotated Statutes §§ 452.400-4-2 | Upon death of parent (child of grandparent) or during divorce, separation, annulment or child custody proceedings between parents. |
| Montana | Montana Code Annotated §§ 40-9-101102 | Circumstances under which grandparent visitation could be obtained are unspecified. |
| Nebraska | Nebraska Revised Statutes §§ 43-1801-1803 | Upon death of parent (child of grandparent) or during divorce, separation, annulment or child custody proceedings between parents. |
| Nevada | Nevada Revised Statutes §§ 125A.330-340 | Upon death of parent (child of grandparent) or during divorce, separation, annulment or child custody proceedings between parents. |

| STATE | STATUTE | GENERAL PROVISIONS |
|-------|---------|-------------------|
| New Hampshire | New Hampshire Revised Statutes Annotated § 458:17 | During divorce, separation, annulment or child custody proceedings between parents. |
| New Jersey | New Jersey Statutes Annotated § 9:2-7.1 | Upon death of parent (child of grandparent) or during divorce, separation, annulment or child custody proceedings between parents. |
| New Mexico | New Mexico Statutes Annotated §§ 40-9-1 to 4 | Upon death of parent (child of grandparent) or during divorce, separation, annulment or child custody proceedings between parents. |
| New York | New York Domestic Relations Law §§ 72, 240(1) | Upon death of parent (child of grandparent) or during divorce, separation, annulment or child custody proceedings between parents, other circumstances under which grandparent visitation could be obtained are unspecified. |
| North Carolina | North Carolina General Statutes §§ 50-13.2(b), 2A, 5(j) | During divorce, separation, annulment or child custody proceedings between parents. |
| North Dakota | North Dakota Cent. Code § 14-09-05.1 | Circumstances under which grandparent visitation could be obtained are unspecified. |
| Ohio | Ohio Revised Code Annotated § 3109.05(B) | During divorce, separation, annulment or child custody proceedings between parents. |
| Oklahoma | Oklahoma Statutes Annotated, Title 10 § 5 | Upon death of parent (child of grandparent) or during divorce, separation, annulment or child custody proceedings between parents; or depending on the amount of time child lived with grandparent. |
| Oregon | Oregon Revised Statutes §§ 109.121-123 | Upon death of parent (child of grandparent) or during divorce, separation, annulment or child custody proceedings between parents. |
| Pennsylvania | 23 Pennsylvania Cons. Statutes Annotated §§ 5311-5314 | Upon death of parent (child of grandparent) or depending on the amount of time child lived with grandparent. |

| STATE | STATUTE | GENERAL PROVISIONS |
|---|---|---|
| Rhode Island | Rhode Island General Laws §§ 15-5-24.1-2 | Upon death of parent (child of grandparent) or during divorce, separation, annulment or child custody proceedings between parents. |
| South Carolina | South Carolina Code Annotated § 20-7-420(33) | Circumstances under which grandparent visitation could be obtained are unspecified. |
| South Dakota | South Dakota Codified Laws Annotated §§ 25-4-52 to 54 | Upon death of parent (child of grandparent) or during divorce, separation, annulment or child custody proceedings between parents. |
| Tennessee | Tennessee Code Annotated § 36-6-3-1 | Circumstances under which grandparent visitation could be obtained are unspecified. |
| Texas | Texas Family code Annotated § 14.03(e)-(g) | Upon death of parent (child of grandparent) or during divorce, separation, annulment or child custody proceedings between parents; or depending on the amount of time child lived with grandparent. |
| Utah | Utah Code Annotated § 30-3-5(4)-(7) | Circumstances under which grandparent visitation could be obtained are unspecified. |
| Vermont | Vermont Statutes Annotated, Title 15 §§ 1011-1016 | Upon death of parent (child of grandparent) or during divorce, separation, annulment or child custody proceedings between parents. |
| Virginia | Virginia Code Annotated § 20-107.2 | During divorce, separation, annulment or child custody proceedings between parents. |
| Washington | Washington Revised Code Annotated § 26.09.240 | Circumstances under which grandparent visitation could be obtained are unspecified. |
| West Virginia | West Virginia Code §§ 48-2-15(b)(1) | Upon death of parent (child of grandparent) or during divorce, separation, annulment or child custody proceedings between parents. |
| Wisconsin | Wisconsin Statutes Annotated § 767.245 | Circumstances under which grandparent visitation could be obtained are unspecified. |

| STATE | STATUTE | GENERAL PROVISIONS |
|-------|---------|--------------------|
| Wyoming | Wyoming Statutes § 20-2-113(c) | Upon death of parent (child of grandparent) or during divorce, separation, annulment or child custody proceedings between parents. |

# APPENDIX 8:
# AMERICAN BAR ASSOCIATION
# POLICY RESOLUTION ON
# GRANDPARENT VISITATION

## RECOMMENDATION

Be it resolved that the American Bar Association encourages the further development of state law on grandparent visitation in accordance with the following guidelines:

1. Attorneys, court personnel and other professionals should be encouraged to refer persons involved in grandparent visitation disputes to appropriate mediation services. If possible such referrals should be made prior to the filing of any court action. Such mediation services should strive to develop agreements between the disputants regarding grandparent visitation, to reduce acrimony between the parties and to minimize any trauma for the child involved.

2. If the parties to a grandparent visitation dispute are unable to resolve the dispute prior to filing a court action, judges presiding in such cases should be encouraged to refer the parties to mediation. Such referrals to mediation should be made, upon motion by a party or "*sua sponte*," if the judge determines that mediation may result in a satisfactory settlement of the dispute.

3. State legislatures should enumerate specific factors for courts to consider in determining whether grandparent visitation is in a child's best interest, including such factors as the following:

(a) The nature and quality of the relationship between the grandparent and the child, including such factors as whether emotional bonds have been established and whether the grandparent has enhanced or interfered with the parent-child relationship;

(b) Whether visitation will promote or disrupt the child's psychological development;

(c) Whether visitation will create friction between the child and his or her parent(s);

(d) Whether visitation will provide support and stability for the child after a nuclear family disruption;

(e) The capacity of the adults involved for future compromise and cooperation in matters involving the child;

(f) The child's wishes, if the child is able to freely form and express a preference; and

(g) Any other factor relevant to a fair and just determination regarding visitation.

State legislation or court rules should require judges presiding in grandparent visitation cases to appoint qualified guardians ad litem for the children involved in such disputes.

# APPENDIX 9:
# UNIFORM CHILD CUSTODY JURISDICTION ACT

## SECTION 1. PURPOSES OF ACT; CONSTRUCTION OF PROVISIONS.

(a) The general purposes of this Act are to:

(1) avoid jurisdictional competition and conflict with courts of other states in matters of child custody which have in the past resulted in the shifting of children from state to state with harmful effects on their well-being;

(2) promote cooperation with the courts of other states to the end that a custody decree is rendered in that state which can best decide the case in the interest of the child;

(3) assure that litigation concerning the custody of a child take place ordinarily in the state with which the child and his family have the closest connection and where significant evidence concerning his care, protection, training, and personal relationships is most readily available, and the courts of this state decline the exercise of jurisdiction when the child and his family have a closer connection with another state;

(4) discourage continuing controversies over child custody in the interest of greater stability of home environment and of secure family relationships for the child;

(5) deter abductions and other unilateral removals of children undertaken to obtain custody awards;

(6) avoid re-litigation of custody decisions of other states in this state insofar as feasible;

(7) facilitate the enforcement of custody decrees of other states;

(8) promote and expand the exchange of information and other forms of mutual assistance between the courts of this state and those of other states concerned with the same child; and

(9) make uniform the law of those states which enact it.

(b) this Act shall be construed to promote the general purposes stated in this section.

## SECTION 2. DEFINITIONS. AS USED IN THIS ACT:

(1) "contestant" means a person, including a parent, who claims a right to custody or visitation rights with respect to a child;

(2) "custody determination" means a court decision and court orders and instructions providing for the custody of a child, including visitation rights; it does not include a decision relating to child support or any other monetary obligation of any person;

(3) "custody proceeding" includes proceedings in which a custody determination is one of several issues, such as an action for divorce or separation, and includes child neglect and dependency proceedings;

(4) "decree" or "custody decree" means a custody determination contained in a judicial decree or order made in a custody proceeding, and includes an initial decree and a modification decree;

(5) "home state" means the state in which the child immediately preceding the time involved lived with his parents, a parent, or a person acting as parent, for at least 6 consecutive months, and in the case of a child less than 6 months old the state in which the child lived from birth with any of the persons mentioned. Periods of temporary absence of any of the named persons are counted as part of the 6-month or other period;

(6) "initial decree" means the first custody decree concerning a particular child;

(7) "modification decree" means a custody decree which modifies or replaces a prior decree, whether made by the court which rendered the prior decree or by another court;

(8) "physical custody" means actual possession and control of a child;

(9) "person acting as parent" means a person, other than a parent, who has physical custody of a child and who has either been awarded custody by a court or claims a right to custody; and

(10) "state" means any state, territory, or possession of the United States, the Commonwealth of Puerto Rico, and the District of Columbia.

* * *

## SECTION 7. INCONVENIENT FORUM.

(a) A court which has jurisdiction under this Act to make an initial or modification decree may decline to exercise its jurisdiction any time before making a decree if it finds that it is an inconvenient forum to make a custody determination under the circumstances of the case and that a court of another State is a more appropriate forum;

(b) A finding of inconvenient forum may be made upon the court's own motion or upon motion of a party or a guardian ad litem or other representative of the child;

(c) In determining if it is an inconvenient forum, the court shall consider if it is in the interest of the child that another state assume jurisdiction. For this purpose it may take into account the following factors, among others:

(1) if another state is or recently was the child's home state;

(2) if another state has a closer connection with the child and his family or with the child and one or more of the contestants;

(3) if substantial evidence concerning the child's present or future care, protection, training, and personal relationships is more readily available in another state;

(4) if the parties have agreed on another forum which is no less appropriate; and

(5) if the exercise of jurisdiction by a court of this State would contravene any of the purposes stated in section 1.

(d) Before determining whether to decline or retain jurisdiction the court may communicate with a court of another state and exchange information pertinent to the assumption of jurisdiction by either court with a view to assuring that jurisdiction will be exercised by the appropriate court and that a forum will be available to the parties.

(e) If the court finds that it is an inconvenient forum and that a court of another state is a more appropriate forum, it may dismiss the proceedings, or it may stay the proceedings upon condition that a custody proceeding be promptly commenced in another named state or upon any other conditions which may be just and proper; including the condition that a moving party stipulate his consent and submission to the jurisdiction of the other forum.

(f) The court may decline to exercise its jurisdiction under this Act if a custody determination is incidental to an action for divorce or another proceeding while retaining jurisdiction of the other forum.

(g) If it appears to the court that it is clearly an inappropriate forum it may require the party who commenced the proceedings to pay, in addition to the costs of the proceedings in this State, necessary travel and other expenses, including attorney's fees, incurred by other parties or their witnesses. Payment is to be made to the clerk of the court for remittance to the proper party.

(h) Upon dismissal or stay of proceedings under this section the court shall inform the court found to be the more appropriate forum of this fact, or if the court which would have jurisdiction in the other state is not certainly known, shall transmit the information to the court administrator or other appropriate official for forwarding to the appropriate party.

(i) Any communication received from another state informing this State of a finding of inconvenient forum because this State is the more appropriate forum shall be filed in the custody registry of the appropriate court. Upon assuming jurisdiction the court of this State shall inform the original court of this fact.

### SECTION 8. JURISDICTION DECLINED BY REASON OF CONDUCT.

(a) If the petitioner for an initial decree has wrongfully taken the child from another state or has engaged in similar reprehensible conduct the court may decline to exercise jurisdiction if this is just and proper under the circumstances.

(b) Unless required in the interest of the child, the court shall not exercise its jurisdiction to modify a custody decree of another state if the petitioner, without consent of the person entitled to custody, has improperly removed the child from the physical custody of the person entitled to custody or has improperly retained the child after a visit or other temporary relinquishment of physical custody. If the petitioner has violated any other provision of a custody decree of another state the court may decline to exercise its jurisdiction if this is just and proper under the circumstances.

(c) In appropriate cases a court dismissing a petition under this section may charge the petitioner with necessary travel and other expenses, including attorney's fees, incurred by other parties or their witnesses.

### SECTION 9. INFORMATION UNDER OATH TO BE SUBMITTED TO THE COURT.

(a) Every party in a custody proceeding in his first pleading or in an affidavit attached to that pleading shall give information under oath as to the child's present address, the places where the child has lived within the last 5 years, and the names and present addresses of the person with whom the child has lived during that period. In this pleading or affidavit every party shall further declare under oath whether:

(1) he has participated (as a party, witness, or in any other capacity) in any other litigation concerning the custody of the same child in this or any other state;

(2) he has information of any custody proceeding concerning the child pending in a court of this or any other state; and

(3) he knows of any person not a party to the proceedings who has physical custody of the child or claims to have custody or visitation with respect to the child.

(b) If the declaration as to any of the above items is in the affirmative the declarant shall give additional information under oath as to details of the information furnished and as to other matters pertinent to the court's jurisdiction and the disposition of the case.

(c) Each party has a continuing duty to inform the court of any custody proceeding concerning the child in this or any other state of which he obtained information during this proceeding.

## SECTION 10. ADDITIONAL PARTIES.

If the court learns from information furnished by the parties pursuant to section 9 or from other sources that a person not a party to the custody proceeding has physical custody of the child or claims to have custody or visitation rights with respect to the child, it shall order that person to be joined as a party and to be duly notified of the pendency of the proceeding and of his joinder as a party. If the person joined as a party is outside this State he shall be served with process or otherwise notified in accordance with section 5.

## SECTION 11. APPEARANCE OF PARTIES AND THE CHILD.

(a) The court may order any party to the proceeding who is in this State to appear personally before the court. If that party has physical custody of the child the court may order that he appear personally with the child.

(b) If a party to the proceeding whose presence is desired by the court is outside this State with or without the child the court may order that the notice given under section 5 include a statement directing that party to appear personally with or without the child declaring that failure to appear may result in a decision adverse to that party.

(c) If a party to the proceeding who is outside this State is directed to appear under subsection (b) or desires to appear personally before the court with or without the child, the court may require another party to pay to the clerk of the court travel and other necessary expenses of the party so appearing and of the child if this is just and proper under the circumstances.

## SECTION 12. BINDING FORCE AND RES JUDICATA EFFECT OF CUSTODY DECREE.

A custody decree rendered by a court of this State which had jurisdiction under section 3 binds all parties who have been served in this State or notified in accordance with section 5 or who have submitted to the jurisdiction of the court, and who have been given an opportunity to be heard. As to these parties the custody decree is conclusive as to all issues of law and fact decided and as to the custody determination made unless and until that determination is modified pursuant to law, including the provisions of this Act.

## SECTION 13. RECOGNITION OF OUT-OF-STATE CUSTODY DECREE.

The courts of this State shall recognize and enforce an initial or modification decree of a court of another state which had assumed jurisdiction under statutory provisions substantially in accordance with this Act or which was made under factual circumstances meeting the jurisdiction standards of the Act, so long as this decree has not been modified in accordance with jurisdictional standards substantially similar to those of this Act.

## SECTION 14. MODIFICATION OF CUSTODY DECREE OF ANOTHER STATE.

(a) If a court of another state has made a custody decree, a court of this State shall not modify that decree unless (1) it appears to the court of this State that the court which rendered the decree does not now have jurisdiction under jurisdictional prerequisites substantially in accordance with this Act or has declined to assume jurisdiction to modify the decree and (2) the court of this State has jurisdiction.

(b) If a court of this State is authorized under subsection (a) and section 8 to modify a custody decree of another state it shall give due consideration to the transcript of the record and other documents of all previous proceedings submitted to it in accordance with section 22.

## SECTION 15. FILING AND ENFORCEMENT OF CUSTODY DECREE OF ANOTHER STATE.

(a) A certified copy of a custody decree of another state may be filed in the office of the clerk of any [District Court, Family Court] of this State.

The clerk shall treat the decree in the same manner as a custody decree of the [District Court, Family Court] of this State. A custody decree so filed has the same effect and shall be enforced in like manner as a custody decree rendered by a court of this State.

(b) A person violating a custody decree of another state which makes it necessary to enforce the decree in this State may be required to pay necessary travel and other expenses, including attorneys' fees, incurred by the party entitled to the custody or his witnesses.

### SECTION 16. REGISTRY OF OUT-OF-STATE CUSTODY DECREES AND PROCEEDINGS.

The clerk of each [District Court, Family Court] shall maintain a registry in which he shall enter the following:

(1) certified copies of custody decrees of other states received for filing;

(2) communications as to the pendency of custody proceedings in other states;

(3) communications concerning a finding of inconvenient forum by a court of another state; and

(4) other communications or documents concerning custody proceedings in another state which may affect the jurisdiction of a court of this State or the disposition to be made by it in a custody proceeding.

### SECTION 17. CERTIFIED COPIES OF CUSTODY DECREE.

The Clerk of the [District Court, Family Court] of this State, at the request of the court of another state or at the request of any person who is affected by or has a legitimate interest in a custody decree, shall certify and forward a copy of the decree to that court or person.

### SECTION 18. TAKING TESTIMONY IN ANOTHER STATE.

In addition to other procedural devices available to a party, any party to the proceeding or a guardian ad litem or other representative of the child may adduce testimony of witnesses, including parties and the child, by deposition or otherwise, in another state. The court on its own motion may direct that the testimony of a person be taken in another state and may prescribe the manner in which and the terms upon which the testimony shall be taken.

## SECTION 19. HEARING AND STUDIES IN ANOTHER STATE; ORDERS TO APPEAL.

(a) A court of this State may request the appropriate court of another state to hold a hearing to adduce evidence, to order a party to produce or give evidence under other procedures of that state, or to have social studies made with respect to the custody of a child involved in proceedings pending in the court of this State; and to forward to the court of this State certified copies of the transcript of the record of the hearing, the evidence otherwise adduced, or any social studies prepared in compliance with the request. The cost of the services may be assessed against the parties or if necessary, ordered paid by the [County, State].

(b) A court of this State may request the appropriate court of another state to order a party to custody proceedings pending in the court of this State to appear in the proceedings, and if that party has physical custody of the child, to appear with the child. The request may state that travel and other necessary expenses of the party and of the child whose appearance is desired will be assessed against another party or will otherwise be paid.

## SECTION 20. ASSISTANCE TO COURTS OF OTHER STATES.

(a) Upon request of the court of another state the courts of this State which are competent to hear custody matters may offer a person in this State to appear at a hearing to adduce evidence or to produce or give evidence under other procedures available in this State [or may order social studies to be made for use in a custody proceeding in another state]. A certified copy of the transcript of the record of the hearing or the evidence otherwise adduced [and any social studies prepared] shall be forwarded by the clerk of the court to the requesting court.

(b) A person within this State may voluntarily give his testimony or statement in this State for use in a custody proceeding outside this State.

(c) Upon request of the court of another state a competent court of this State may order a person in this State to appear alone or with the child in a custody proceeding in another state. The court may condition compliance with the request upon assurance by the other state that state travel and other necessary expenses will be advanced or reimbursed.

## SECTION 21. PRESERVATION OF DOCUMENTS FOR USE IN OTHER STATES.

In any custody proceeding in this State the court shall preserve the pleadings, orders and decrees, any record that has been made of its hearing, social studies, and other pertinent documents until the child reaches [18, 21] years of age. Upon appropriate request of the court of another state the court shall forward to the other court certified copies of any or all of such documents.

## SECTION 22. REQUEST FOR COURT RECORDS OF ANOTHER STATE.

If a custody decree has been rendered in another state concerning a child involved in a custody proceeding pending in a court of this State, the court of this State upon taking jurisdiction of the case shall request of the court record and other documents mentioned in section 21.

## SECTION 23. INTERNATIONAL APPLICATION.

The general policies of this Act extend to the international area. The provisions of this Act relating to the recognition and enforcement of custody decrees of other states apply to custody decrees and decrees involving legal institutions similar in nature to custody institutions rendered by appropriate authorities of other nations if reasonable notice and opportunity to be heard were given to all affected persons.

## SECTION 24. PRIORITY.

Upon the request of a party to a custody proceeding which raises a question of existence or exercise of jurisdiction under this Act the case shall be given calendar priority and handled expeditiously.

## SECTION 25. SEVERABILITY.

If any provisions of this Act or the application thereof to any person or circumstance is held invalid, its invalidity does not affect other provisions or applications of the Act which can be given effect without the invalid provision or application, and to this end the provisions of this Act are severable.

## SECTION 26. SHORT TITLE.

This Act may be cited as the Uniform Child Custody Jurisdiction Act.

## SECTION 27. REPEAL.

The following acts and parts of acts are repealed:

[State to provide]

## SECTION 28. TIME OF TAKING EFFECT.

[State to provide]

# APPENDIX 10:
# PARENTAL KIDNAPPING
# PREVENTION ACT OF 1980

**28 U.S.C. §1738A. FULL FAITH AND CREDIT GIVEN TO CHILD CUSTODY DETERMINATIONS**

**(a)** The appropriate authorities of every State shall enforce according to its terms, and shall not modify except as provided in subsection (f) of this section, any child custody determination made consistently with the provisions of this section by a court of another State.

**(b)** As used in this section, the term—

(1) "child" means a person under the age of eighteen;

(2) "contestant" means a person, including a parent, who claims a right to custody or visitation of a child;

(3) "custody determination" means a judgment, decree, or other order of a court providing for the custody or visitation of a child, and includes permanent and temporary orders, and initial orders and modifications;

(4) "home State" means the State in which, immediately preceding the time involved, the child lived with his parents, a parent, or a person acting as parent, for at least six consecutive months, and in the case of a child less than six months old, the State in which the child lived from birth with any of such persons. Periods of temporary absence of any of such persons are counted as part of the six-month or other period;

(5) "modification" and "modify" refer to a custody determination which modifies, replaces, supersedes, or otherwise is made subsequent to, a prior custody determination concerning the same child, whether made by the same court or not;

(6) "person acting as a parent" means a person, other than a parent, who has physical custody of a child and who has either been awarded custody by a court or claims a right to custody;

(7) "physical custody" means actual possession and control of a child; and

(8) "State" means a State of the United States, the District of Columbia, the Commonwealth of Puerto Rico, or a territory or possession of the United States.

(c) A child custody determination made by a court of a State is consistent with the provisions of this section only if—

(1) such court has jurisdiction under the law of such State; and

(2) one of the following conditions is met:

(A) such State (i) is the home State of the child on the date of the commencement of the proceeding, or (ii) had been the child's home State within six months before the date of the commencement of the proceeding and the child is absent from such State because of his removal or retention by a contestant or for other reasons, and a contestant continues to live in such State;

(B)(i) it appears that no other State would have jurisdiction under subparagraph (A), and (ii) it is in the best interest of the child that a court of such State assume jurisdiction because (I) the child and his parents, or the child and at least one contestant, have a significant connection with such State other than mere physical presence in such State and (II) there is available in such state substantial evidence concerning the child's present or future care, protection, training, and personal relationships;

(C) the child is physically present in such State and (i) the child has been abandoned, or (ii) it is necessary in an emergency to protect the child because he has been subjected to or threatened with mistreatment or abuse;

(D) (i) it appears that no other State would have jurisdiction under subparagraph (A), (B), (C), or (E), or another State has declined to exercise jurisdiction on the ground that the State whose jurisdiction is in issue is the more appropriate forum to determine the custody of the child, and (ii) it is in the best interest of the child that such court assume jurisdiction; or

(E) the court has continuing jurisdiction pursuant to subsection (d).

(d) The jurisdiction of a court of a State which has made a custody determination consistently with the provisions of this section continues as long as the requirement of subsection (c)(l) continues to be met and such State remains the residence of the child or of any contestant.

(e) Before a child custody determination is made, reasonable notice and opportunity to be heard shall be given to the contestants, any parent whose parental rights have not been previously terminated and any person who has physical custody of a child.

(f) A court of a State may modify a determination of the custody of the same child made by a court of another State, if—

(1) it has jurisdiction to make a child custody determination; and

(2) the court of the other State no longer has jurisdiction, or it has declined to exercise such jurisdiction to modify such determination.

(g) A court of a State shall not exercise jurisdiction in any proceeding for a custody determination commenced during the pendency of a proceeding in a court of another State where such court of that other State is exercising jurisdiction consistently with the provisions of this section to make a custody determination.

# APPENDIX 11:
# JURISDICTIONS THAT HAVE ENACTED THE UNIFORM CHILD-CUSTODY JURISDICTION AND ENFORCEMENT ACT (UCCJEA)

ALABAMA
ALASKA
ARIZONA
ARKANSAS
CALIFORNIA
COLORADO
CONNECTICUT
DELAWARE
DISTRICT OF COLUMBIA
FLORIDA
GEORGIA
HAWAII
IDAHO
ILLINOIS
IOWA
KANSAS
KENTUCKY
MAINE
MARYLAND
MICHIGAN
MINNESOTA

MISSISSIPPI
MONTANA
NEBRASKA
NEVADA
NEW JERSEY
NEW MEXICO
NEW YORK
NORTH CAROLINA
NORTH DAKOTA
OHIO
OKLAHOMA
OREGON
PENNSYLVANIA
RHODE ISLAND
TENNESSEE
TEXAS
UTAH
VIRGINIA
WASHINGTON
WEST VIRGINIA

SOURCE: U.S. Department of Justice.

# APPENDIX 12:
# SAMPLE PETITION FOR CUSTODY OR
# VISITATION UNDER THE UCCJEA

DRL Art. 5-A

Form UCCJEA-1
(Petition-Custody,
Visitation–UCCJEA)
10/2004

FAMILY COURT OF THE STATE OF NEW YORK
COUNTY OF
.......................................................................................

In The Matter of a Proceeding for
❏ Custody ❏ Visitation under the *Uniform Custody*
*Jurisdiction and Enforcement Act*

Docket No.

               Petitioner

PETITION–UCCJEA
❏ CUSTODY
❏ VISITATION

     -against-

               Respondent
.......................................................................................

TO THE FAMILY COURT:

The undersigned Petitioner respectfully alleges upon information and belief that:

     1. I am [specify relationship to child; if foster parent, agency, institution or other relationship, so state]:         and am seeking an order of [check applicable box(es)]:
❏ custody ❏ visitation regarding [specify child's name]:
I [check applicable box]: ❏ reside ❏ am located at [specify address or indicate if ordered to be kept confidential pursuant to Family Court Act §154-b(2) or Domestic Relations Law §254]:

     2. Respondent [specify name]:     is [specify relationship to child; if foster parent, agency, institution or other relationship, so state]:
Respondent [check applicable box]: ❏ resides ❏ is located at [specify address or indicate if ordered to be kept confidential pursuant to Family Court Act §154-b(2) or Domestic Relations Law §254]:

     3. The name, present address and date of birth of each child who is the subject of this proceeding are as follows [specify address or indicate if ordered to be kept confidential pursuant to Family Court Act §154-b(2) or Domestic Relations Law §254] :

| Name | Address | Date of Birth |
|------|---------|---------------|

     4. This Court has jurisdiction to issue a child custody or visitation order pursuant to Section 76(1) of the Domestic Relations Law on the following ground(s) [check all applicable box(es)]:

     a. ❏  this state is the home state of the child on the date of the filing of this petition;
        ❏  this state was the home state of the child within six months before the filing of this petition; and the child is absent from this state but the following parent or

person acting  as a parent continues to live in this state [specify]:                    ;
OR

b. ❑   the child and the child's parents, or the child and at least one parent or a person acting as a parent, have a significant connection with this state other than mere physical presence; and  substantial evidence is available in this state concerning the child's care, protection, training, and personal relationships; and EITHER [check applicable box]:    ❑ a court of another state does not have home state jurisdiction under paragraph (a); OR

❑ a court of the home state of the child [check applicable box]:  ❑ has declined  ❑ should decline to exercise jurisdiction on the  ground that this state is the more appropriate forum under Domestic Relations Law §§76-f or 76-g,  because [specify]:

OR

c.❑   all courts having jurisdiction under paragraph (a) or (b) of this subdivision [check applicable box]:  ❑ have declined  ❑ should decline   to exercise jurisdiction on the ground that a court of this state is the more appropriate forum to determine the custody of the child under Domestic Relations  Law §§76-f or 76-g,  because [specify]:

OR

d.❑   no court of any other state would have jurisdiction under the criteria specified in paragraph (a), (b) or (c).

5.  This Court should exercise temporary, emergency jurisdiction, pursuant to Domestic Relations Law §76-c, because the child is presently in this State and [check one or both boxes]:
❑ the child has been abandoned [specify facts or circumstances]:

❑ it is necessary in an emergency to protect the child, a sibling or parent of the child [specify facts or circumstances]:

6. [Delete if inapplicable]:  An order was issued by                 Court,                County, State of                 , referring the issue of ❑custody  ❑ visitation  to the Family Court of the State of New York in and for the County of [specify]:

7.  Check applicable box(es):
❑ No proceeding has been commenced that could affect this action.
❑ The following proceeding(s) have been commenced that could affect this action, [specify jurisdiction, court, docket or index number, type and status of proceeding]:

❑(Upon information and belief) an order of ❑ custody ❑ visitation of one or more of the same child(ren) has been registered  in  ❑ New York State  ❑ another state, territory, tribal jurisdiction or country [specify court(s) and jurisdiction(s) in which order registered, date of registration(s),  court and jurisdiction that issued the order, children covered by the order and date of order, if available]:

8. [Check applicable box(es). Delete inapplicable provisions]:
a. ❑ The father of the child(ren) who (is)(are) the subject(s) of this proceeding is [specify]:

❑ The father was married to the child(ren)'s mother at the time of the conception or birth.
❑ An order of filiation was made on [specify date and court and attach true copy]:
❑ An acknowledgment of paternity was signed on [specify date]:
by            [specify who signed and attach a true copy]:
❑ The father is deceased.

b. ❑ The father of the child(ren) who (is)(are) the subject(s) of this proceeding has not been legally established.

c. ❑ A paternity agreement or compromise was approved by the Family Court of
County on            ,            , concerning [name parties to agreement or compromise and child(ren) and attach a true copy]:

9. [Applicable to cases in which mother is not a party]: The name and address of the mother is [indicate if deceased or if address ordered to be kept confidential pursuant to Family Court Act §154-b(2) or Domestic Relations Law §254]:

10. During the last five years, each child who is the subject of this proceeding resided at: [specify address or indicate if ordered to be kept confidential pursuant to Family Court Act §154-b(2) or Domestic Relations Law §254]:
Name                    Address                    Duration (from/to)

11. The name and present address of the person(s) with whom each child resided during the past five years are as follows [specify address or indicate if ordered to be kept confidential, pursuant to Family Court Act §154-b(2) or Domestic Relations Law §254]:
Name                    Address                    Duration (from/to)

12. Petitioner ❑ has ❑ has not participated as a ❑ party ❑ witness ❑ other [specify]:
in other litigation concerning the custody of the same child(ren) in ❑ New York State ❑ Other State or other jurisdiction [specify]:                            . If so, specify type of case, capacity of participation, court, location and status of case:

13. [Check applicable box]:
❑ The following person(s) not party to these proceedings have claimed ❑ physical custody or ❑ visitation rights to the child(ren) as follows:

❑ I know of no person(s) not a party to the proceedings who claim(s) to have custody or visitation rights with respect to the child(ren) affected by this proceeding.

14. The custody or visitation of the child(ren) has been determined or agreed upon in the following instruments [specify court, if any, and date and attach true copy of instrument(s)]:
   ❑ Custody order of [specify court and location]:                    , dated [specify]:
   ❑ Stipulation of settlement in [specify court and location]:              , dated [specify]:

   ❑ Judgment of Divorce of [specify court and location]:                  , dated [specify]:
   ❑ Separation Agreement, dated [specify]:

   ❑ Custody or Guardianship Agreement confirmed by [specify court and location]:
      , dated [specify]:
15. Petitioner Respondent obtained custody of the child(ren) on [specify date]: , as follows:


16. It would be in the best interests of the child(ren) for Petitioner to have ❑ custody ❑ visitation for the following reasons [specify]:

17. The following circumstances have changed since entry of the ❑ order ❑ judgment ❑ other [specify]:              of ❑ custody ❑ visitation [specify]:


18. An Order of Protection or Temporary Order of Protection was issued [check applicable box(es]: ❑ against Respondent ❑ against me
in the following criminal, matrimonial or Family Court proceeding(s) [specify the court, docket or index number, date of order, next court date and status of case, if available]:

The ❑ Order of Protection ❑ Temporary Order of Protection expired or will expire on [specify]:

19. Petitioner requests a Temporary Order of Protection pursuant to Family Court Act §655 because [specify]:

20. The subject child(ren) ❑ are ❑ are not Native-American child(ren) subject to the Indian Child Welfare Act of 1978 (25 U.S.C. §§ 1901-1963).

21. No previous application has been made to any court or judge for the relief herein requested, except [specify; delete if inapplicable]:

WHEREFORE, Petitioner respectfully requests this Court to issue:

A. An order awarding ❑ custody ❑ visitation of the above-named child(ren) to the Petitioner as follows [specify]:

B. An order directing the Respondent to appear before the Court immediately with the above-named child(ren) for a hearing;

C. A warrant for the Respondent to appear with the above-named children;

D. An order directing the following temporary, emergency measures to protect the child, a parent or sibling [specify]:

E. An order directing the following measures necessary to ensure the safety of the child and any person ordered to appear [specify]:

F. An order directing the Respondent to pay Petitioner's attorneys' fees and costs, including reasonable and necessary travel expenses, for the prosecution of this proceeding; and

G. A temporary order of protection containing the following condition(s) [specify]:

H. An order directing such other and further relief as the Court may determine to be just and proper.

Dated:

_____
Petitioner

_____
Print or Type Name

_____
Signature of Attorney, if any

_____
Attorney's Name (print or type)

_____
Attorney's Address and Telephone Number

VERIFICATION

STATE OF NEW YORK )
                         :ss:
COUNTY OF              )

being duly sworn, says that (s)he is the Petitioner in the above-named proceeding and that the foregoing petition is true to (his)(her) own knowledge, except as to matters therein stated to be alleged on information and belief and as to those matters (s)he believes it to be true.

_____
Petitioner

Sworn to before me this
    day of

_____
(Deputy) Clerk of the Court
    Notary Public

# APPENDIX 13:
# HAGUE CONVENTION ON THE CIVIL ASPECTS OF INTERNATIONAL CHILD ABDUCTION

The States signatory to the present Convention, firmly convinced that the interests of children are of paramount importance in matters relating to their custody, desiring to protect children internationally from the harmful effects of their wrongful removal or retention and to establish procedures to ensure their prompt return to the State of their habitual residence, as well as to secure protection for rights of access, have resolved to conclude a Convention to this effect, and have agreed upon the following provisions—

## CHAPTER I—SCOPE OF THE CONVENTION

### ARTICLE 1

The objects of the present Convention are—

(a) to secure the prompt return of children wrongfully removed to or retained in any Contracting State, and

(b) to ensure that rights of custody and of access under the law of one Contracting State are effectively respected in other Contracting States.

### ARTICLE 2

Contracting States shall take all appropriate measures to secure within their territories the implementation of the objects of the Convention. For this purpose they shall use the most expeditious procedures available.

## ARTICLE 3

The removal or the retention of a child is to be considered wrongful where—

(a) it is in breach of rights of custody attributed to a person, an institution or any other body, either jointly or alone, under the law of the State in which the child was habitually resident immediately before the removal or retention; and

(b) at the time of removal or retention those rights were actually exercised, either jointly or alone, or would have been so exercised but for the removal or retention. The rights of custody mentioned in sub-paragraph (a) above, may arise in particular by operation of law or by reason of a judicial or administrative decision, or by reason of an agreement having legal effect under the law of that State.

## ARTICLE 4

The Convention shall apply to any child who was habitually resident in a Contracting State immediately before any breach of custody or access rights. The Convention shall cease to apply when the child attains the age of 16 years.

## ARTICLE 5

For the purposes of this Convention—

(a) 'rights of custody' shall include rights relating to the care of the person of the child and, in particular, the right to determine the child's place of residence;

(b) 'rights of access' shall include the right to take a child for a limited period of time to a place other than the child's habitual residence.

## CHAPTER II—CENTRAL AUTHORITIES

## ARTICLE 6

A Contracting State shall designate a Central Authority to discharge the duties which are imposed by the Convention upon such authorities. Federal States, States with more than one system of law or States having autonomous territorial organizations shall be free to appoint more than one Central Authority and to specify the territorial extent of their powers. Where a State has appointed more than one Central Authority, it shall designate the Central Authority to which applications may be addressed for transmission to the appropriate Central Authority within that State.

## ARTICLE 7

Central Authorities shall co-operate with each other and promote co-operation amongst the competent authorities in their respective States to secure the prompt return of children and to achieve the other objects of this Convention. In particular, either directly or through any intermediary, they shall take all appropriate measures—

(a) to discover the whereabouts of a child who has been wrongfully removed or retained;

(b) to prevent further harm to the child or prejudice to interested parties by taking or causing to be taken provisional measures;

(c) to secure the voluntary return of the child or to bring about an amicable resolution of the issues;

(d) to exchange, where desirable, information relating to the social background of the child;

(e) to provide information of a general character as to the law of their State in connection with the application of the Convention;

(f) to initiate or facilitate the institution of judicial or administrative proceedings with a view to obtaining the return of the child and, in a proper case, to make arrangements for organizing or securing the effective exercise of rights of access;

(g) where the circumstances so require, to provide or facilitate the provision of legal aid and advice, including the participation of legal counsel and advisers;

(h) to provide such administrative arrangements as may be necessary and appropriate to secure the safe return of the child;

(i) to keep other each other informed with respect to the operation of this Convention and, as far as possible, to eliminate any obstacles to its application.

## CHAPTER III—RETURN OF CHILDREN

## ARTICLE 8

Any person, institution or other body claiming that a child has been removed or retained in breach of custody rights may apply either to the Central Authority of the child's habitual residence or to the Central Authority of any other Contracting State for assistance in securing the return of the child.

The application shall contain—

(a) information concerning the identity of the applicant, of the child and of the person alleged to have removed or retained the child;

(b) where available, the date of birth of the child;

(c) the grounds on which the applicant's claim for return of the child is based;

(d) all available information relating to the whereabouts of the child and the identity of the person with whom the child is presumed to be.

The application may be accompanied or supplemented by—

(e) an authenticated copy of any relevant decision or agreement;

(f) a certificate or an affidavit emanating from a Central Authority, or other competent authority of the State of the child's habitual residence, or from a qualified person, concerning the relevant law of that State;

(g) any other relevant document.

## ARTICLE 9

If the Central Authority which receives an application referred to in Article 8 has reason to believe that the child is in another Contracting State, it shall directly and without delay transmit the application to the Central Authority of that Contracting State and inform the requesting Central Authority, or the applicant, as the case may be.

## ARTICLE 10

The Central Authority of the State where the child is shall take or cause to be taken all appropriate measures in order to obtain the voluntary return of the child.

## ARTICLE 11

The judicial or administrative authorities of Contracting States shall act expeditiously in proceedings for the return of children.

If the judicial or administrative authority concerned has not reached a decision within six weeks from the date of commencement of the proceedings, the applicant or the Central Authority of the requested State, on its own initiative or if asked by the Central Authority of the requesting State, shall have the right to request a statement of the reasons for the delay. If a reply is received by the Central Authority of the requested State, that Authority shall transmit the reply to the Central Authority of the requesting State, or to the applicant, as the case may be.

## ARTICLE 12

Where a child has been wrongfully removed or retained in terms of Article 3 and, at the date of the commencement of the proceedings before the judicial or administrative authority of the Contracting State where the child is, a period of less than one year has elapsed from the date of the wrongful removal or retention, the authority concerned shall order the return of the child forthwith.

The judicial or administrative authority, even where the proceedings have been commenced after the expiration of the period of one year referred to in the preceding paragraph, shall also order the return of the child, unless it is demonstrated that the child is now settled in its new environment.

Where the judicial or administrative authority in the requested State has reason to believe that the child has been taken to another State, it may stay the proceedings or dismiss the application for the return of the child.

## ARTICLE 13

Notwithstanding the provisions of the preceding Article, the judicial or administrative authority of the requested State is not bound to order the return of the child if the person, institution or other body which opposes its return establishes that—

(a) the person, institution or other body having the care of the person of the child was not actually exercising the custody rights at the time of removal or retention, or had consented to or subsequently acquiesced in the removal or retention; or

(b) there is a grave risk that his or her return would expose the child to physical or psychological harm or otherwise place the child in an intolerable situation.

The judicial or administrative authority may also refuse to order the return of the child if it finds that the child objects to being returned and has attained an age and degree of maturity at which it is appropriate to take account of its views.

In considering the circumstances referred to in this Article, the judicial and administrative authorities shall take into account the information relating to the social background of the child provided by the Central

Authority or other competent authority of the child's habitual residence.

## ARTICLE 14

In ascertaining whether there has been a wrongful removal of retention within the meaning of Article 3, the judicial or administrative authorities of the requested State may take notice directly of the law of, and of judicial or administrative decisions, formally recognized or not in the State of the habitual residence of the child, without recourse to the specific procedures for the proof of that law or for the recognition of foreign decisions which would otherwise be applicable.

## ARTICLE 15

The judicial or administrative authorities of a Contracting State may, prior to the making of an order for the return of the child, request that the applicant obtain from the authorities of the State of the habitual residence of the child a decision or other determination that the removal or retention was wrongful within the meaning of Article 3 of the Convention, where such a decision or determination may be obtained in that State. The Central Authorities of the Contracting States shall so far as practicable assist applicants to obtain such a decision or determination.

## ARTICLE 16

After receiving notice of a wrongful removal or retention of a child in the sense of Article 3, the judicial or administrative authorities of the Contracting State to which the child has been removed or in which it has been retained shall not decide on the merits of rights of custody until it has been determined that the child is not to be returned under this Convention or unless an application under the Convention is not lodged within a reasonable time following receipt of the notice.

## ARTICLE 17

The sole fact that a decision relating to custody has been given in or is entitled to recognition in the requested State shall not be a ground for refusing to return a child under this Convention, but the judicial or administrative authorities of the requested State may take account of the reasons for that decision in applying this Convention.

## ARTICLE 18

The provisions of this Chapter do not limit the power of a judicial or administrative authority to order the return of the child at any time.

## ARTICLE 19

A decision under this Convention concerning the return of the child shall not be taken to be determination on the merits of any custody issue.

## ARTICLE 20

The return of the child under the provision of Article 12 may be refused if this would not be permitted by the fundamental principles of the requested State relating to the protection of human rights and fundamental freedoms.

# CHAPTER IV—RIGHTS OF ACCESS

## ARTICLE 21

An application to make arrangements for organizing or securing the effective exercise of rights of access may be presented to the Central Authorities of the Contracting States in the same way as an application for the return of a child.

The Central Authorities are bound by the obligations of co-operation which are set forth in Article 7 to promote the peaceful enjoyment of access rights and the fulfillment of any conditions to which the exercise of such rights may be subject. The Central Authorities shall take steps to remove, as far as possible, all obstacles to the exercise of such rights. The Central Authorities, either directly or through intermediaries, may initiate or assist in the institution of proceedings with a view to organizing or protecting these rights and securing respect for the conditions to which the exercise of these rights may be subject.

# CHAPTER V—GENERAL PROVISIONS

## ARTICLE 22

No security, bond or deposit, however described, shall be required to guarantee the payment of costs and expenses in the judicial or administrative proceedings falling within the scope of this Convention.

## ARTICLE 23

No legalization or similar formality may be required in the context of this Convention.

## ARTICLE 24

Any application, communication or other document sent to the Central Authority of the requested State shall be in the original language, and shall be accompanied by a translation into the official language or one of the official languages of the requested State or, where that is not feasible, a translation into French or English.

However, a Contracting State may, by making a reservation in accordance with Article 42, object to the use of either French or English, but not both, in any application, communication or other document sent to its Central Authority.

## ARTICLE 25

Nationals of the Contracting States and persons who are habitually resident within those States shall be entitled in matters concerned with the application of this Convention to legal aid and advice in any other Contracting State on the same conditions as if they themselves were nationals of and habitually resident in that State.

## ARTICLE 26

Each Central Authority shall bear its own costs in applying this Convention. Central Authorities and other public services of Contracting States shall not impose any charges in relation to applications submitted under this Convention. In particular, they may not require any payment from the applicant towards the costs and expenses of the proceedings or, where applicable, those arising from the participation of legal counsel or advisers.

However, they may require the payment of the expenses incurred or to be incurred in implementing the return of the child.

However, a Contracting State may, by making a reservation in accordance with Article 42, declare that it shall not be bound to assume any costs referred to in the preceding paragraph resulting from the participation of legal counsel or advisers or from court proceedings, except insofar as those costs may be covered by its system of legal aid and advice.

Upon ordering the return of a child or issuing an order concerning rights of access under this Convention, the judicial or administrative authorities may, where appropriate, direct the person who removed or retained the child, or who prevented the exercise of rights of access, to pay necessary expenses incurred by or on behalf of the applicant, including travel expenses, any costs incurred or payments made for locating the child, the costs of legal representation of the applicant, and those of returning the child.

## ARTICLE 27

When it is manifest that the requirements of this Convention are not fulfilled or that the application is otherwise not well founded, a Central Authority is not bound to accept the application. In that case, the Central Authority shall forthwith inform the applicant or the Central Authority through which the application was submitted, as the case may be, of its reasons.

## ARTICLE 28

A Central Authority may require that the application be accompanied by a written authorization empowering it to act on behalf of the applicant, or to designate a representative so to act.

## ARTICLE 29

This Convention shall not preclude any person, institution or body who claims that there has been a breach of custody or access rights within the meaning of Article 3 or 21 from applying directly to the judicial or administrative authorities of a Contracting State, whether or not under the provisions of this Convention.

## ARTICLE 30

Any application submitted to the Central Authorities or directly to the judicial or administrative authorities of a Contracting State in accordance with the terms of this Convention, together with documents and any other information appended thereto or provided by a Central Authority, shall be admissible in the courts or administrative authorities of the Contracting States.

## ARTICLE 31

In relation to a State which in matters of custody of children has two or more systems of law applicable in different territorial units—

(a) any reference to habitual residence in that State shall be construed as referring to habitual residence in a territorial unit of that State;

(b) any reference to the law of the State of habitual residence shall be construed as referring to the law of the territorial unit in that State where the child habitually resides.

## ARTICLE 32

In relation to a State which in matters of custody of children has two or more systems of law applicable to different categories of persons, any reference to the law of that State shall be construed as referring to the legal system specified by the law of that State.

## ARTICLE 33

A State within which different territorial units have their own rules of law in respect of custody of children shall not be bound to apply this Convention where a State with a unified system of law would not be bound to do so.

## ARTICLE 34

This Convention shall take priority in matters within its scope over the Convention of 5 October 1961 concerning the powers of authorities and the law applicable in respect of the protection of minors, as between Parties to both Conventions. Otherwise the present Convention shall not restrict the application of an international instrument in force between the State of origin and the State addressed or other law of the State addressed for the purposes of obtaining the return of a child who has been wrongfully removed or retained or of organizing access rights.

## ARTICLE 35

This Convention shall apply as between Contracting States only to wrongful removals or retentions occurring after its entry into force in those States.

Where a declaration has been made under Article 39 or 40, the reference in the preceding paragraph to a Contracting State shall be taken to refer to the territorial unit or units in relation to which this Convention applies.

## ARTICLE 36

Nothing in this Convention shall prevent two or more Contracting State, in order to limit the restrictions to which the return of the child may be subject, from agreeing among themselves to derogate from any provision of this Convention which may imply such a restriction.

# CHAPTER VI—FINAL CLAUSES

## ARTICLE 37

The Convention shall be open for signature by the States which were Members of the Hague Conference on Private International Law at the time of its Fourteenth Session. It shall be ratified, accepted or approved and the instruments of ratification, acceptance or approval shall be deposited with the Ministry of Foreign Affairs of the Kingdom of the Netherlands.

## ARTICLE 38

Any other State may accede to the Convention. The instrument of accession shall be deposited with the Ministry of Foreign Affairs of the Kingdom of the Netherlands.

The Convention shall enter into force for a State acceding to it on the first day of the third calendar month after the deposit of its instrument of accession. The accession will have effect only as regards the relations between the acceding State and such Contracting States as will have declared their acceptance of the accession. Such a declaration will also have to be made by any Member State ratifying, accepting or approving the Convention after an accession. Such declaration shall be deposited at the Ministry of Foreign Affairs of the Kingdom of the Netherlands; this Ministry shall forward, through diplomatic channels, a certified copy to each of the Contracting States.

The Convention will enter into force as between the acceding State and the State that has declared its acceptance of the accession on the first day of the third calendar month after the deposit of the declaration of acceptance.

## ARTICLE 39

Any State may, at the time of signature, ratification, acceptance, approval or accession, declare that the Convention shall extend to all the territories for the international relations of which it is responsible, or to one or more of them. Such a declaration shall take effect at the time the Convention enters into force for that State. Such declaration, as well as any subsequent extension, shall be notified to the Ministry of Foreign Affairs of the Kingdom of the Netherlands.

## ARTICLE 40

If a Contracting State has two or more territorial units in which different systems of law are applicable in relation to matters dealt with in this Convention, it may at the time of signature, ratification, acceptance, approval or accession declare that this Convention shall extend to all its territorial units or only to one or more of them and may modify this declaration by submitting another declaration at any time. Any such declaration shall be notified to the Ministry of Foreign Affairs of the Kingdom of the Netherlands and shall state expressly the territorial units to which the Convention applies.

## ARTICLE 41

Where a Contracting State has a system of government under which executive, judicial and legislative powers are distributed between central and other authorities within that State, its signature or ratification, acceptance or approval of, or accession to this Convention, or its making of any declaration in terms of Article 40 shall carry no implication as to the internal distribution of powers within that State.

## ARTICLE 42

Any State may, not later than the time of ratification, acceptance, approval or accession, or at the time of making a declaration in terms of Article 39 or 40, make one or both of the reservations provided for in Article 24 and Article 26, third paragraph. No other reservations shall be permitted. Any State may at any time withdraw a reservation it has made. The withdraw shall be notified to the Ministry of Foreign Affairs of the Kingdom of the Netherlands. The reservation shall cease to have effect on the first day of the third calendar month after the notification referred to in the preceding paragraph.

## ARTICLE 43

The Convention shall enter into force on the first day of the third calendar month after the deposit of the third instrument of ratification, acceptance, approval or accession referred to in Articles 37 and 38. Thereafter the Convention shall enter into force—

(1) for each State ratifying, accepting, approving or acceding to it subsequently, on the first day of the third calendar month after the deposit of its instrument of ratification, acceptance, approval or accession;

(2) for any territory or territorial unit to which the Convention has been extended in conformity with Article 39 or 40, on the first day of the third calendar month after the notification referred to in that Article.

## ARTICLE 44

The Convention shall remain in force for five years from the date of its entry into force in accordance with the first paragraph of Article 43 even for States which subsequently have ratified, accepted, approved it or acceded to it. If there has been no denunciation, it shall be renewed tacitly every five years. Any denunciation shall be notified to the Ministry of Foreign Affairs of the Kingdom of the Netherlands at least six months before the expiry of the five year period. It may be limited to certain of the territories or territorial units to which the Convention applies.

The denunciation shall have effect only as regards the State which has notified it. The Convention shall remain in force for the other Contracting States.

## ARTICLE 45

The Ministry of Foreign Affairs of the Kingdom of the Netherlands shall notify the States Members of the Conference, and the States which have acceded in accordance with Article 38, of the following—

(1) the signatures and ratifications, acceptances and approvals referred to in Article 37;

(2) the accession referred to in Article 38;

(3) the date on which the Convention enters into force in accordance with Article 43;

(4) the extensions referred to in Article 39;

(5) the declarations referred to in Articles 38 and 40;

(6) the reservations referred to in Article 24 and Article 26, third paragraph, and the withdrawals referred to in Article 42;

(7) the denunciation referred to in Article 44.

In witness whereof the undersigned, being duly authorized thereto, have signed this Convention.

Done at The Hague, on the 25th day of October, 1980, in the English and French languages, both texts being equally authentic, in a single copy which shall be deposited in the archives of the Government of the Kingdom of the Netherlands, and of which a certified copy shall be sent, through diplomatic channels, to each of the States Members of the Hague Conference on Private International Law at the date of its Fourteenth Session.

# APPENDIX 14:
# PARTIES TO THE HAGUE CONVENTION

| COUNTRY | ENTRY DATE |
|---|---|
| ARGENTINA | June 1, 1991 |
| AUSTRALIA | July 1, 1988 |
| AUSTRIA | October 1, 1988 |
| BAHAMAS | January 1, 1994 |
| BELGIUM | May 1, 1999 |
| BELIZE | November 1, 1989 |
| BERMUDA | March 1, 1999 |
| BOSNIA AND HERZEGOVINA | December 1, 1991 |
| BRAZIL | December 1, 2003 |
| BULGARIA | January 1, 2005 |
| BURKINA FASO | November 1, 1992 |
| CANADA | July 1, 1988 |
| CAYMAN ISLANDS | August 1, 1998 |
| CHILE | July 1, 1994 |
| CHINA | (Hong Kong Special Admin. Region-September 1, 1997); (Macau-March 1, 1999) |
| COLOMBIA | June 1, 1996 |
| CROATIA | December 1, 1991 |
| CZECH REPUBLIC | March 1, 1998 |
| CYPRUS | March 1, 1995 |
| DENMARK | July 1, 1991 |
| ECUADOR | April 1, 1992 |
| FINLAND | August 1, 1994 |
| FRANCE | July 1, 1988 |

| COUNTRY | ENTRY DATE |
|---------|-----------|
| GERMANY | December 1, 1990 |
| GREECE | June 1, 1993 |
| HONDURAS | June 1, 1994 |
| HUNGARY | Jul 1, 1988 |
| ICELAND | December 1, 1996 |
| IRELAND | October 1, 1991 |
| ISLE OF MAN | September 1, 1991 |
| ISRAEL | December 1, 1991 |
| ITALY | May 1, 1995 |
| LUXEMBOURG | July 1, 1988 |
| MACEDONIA, FORMER YUGOSLAV REPUBLIC OF | December 1, 1991 |
| MALTA | February 1, 2003 |
| MAURITIUS | October 1, 1993 |
| MEXICO | October 1, 1991 |
| MONACO | June 1, 1993 |
| MONTSERRAT | March 1, 1999 |
| NETHERLANDS | September 1, 1990 |
| NEW ZEALAND | October 1, 1991 |
| NORWAY | April 1, 1989 |
| PANAMA | June 1, 1994 |
| POLAND | November 1, 1992 |
| PORTUGAL | July 1, 1988 |
| ROMANIA | June 1, 1993 |
| SLOVAK REPUBLIC | February 1, 2001 |
| OSLOVENIA | April 1, 1995 |
| SOUTH AFRICA | November 1, 1997 |
| SPAIN | July 1, 1988 |
| ST. KITTS AND NEVIS | June 1, 1995 |
| SWEDEN | June 1, 1989 |
| SWITZERLAND | July 1, 1988 |
| TURKEY | August 1, 2000 |

| COUNTRY | ENTRY DATE |
| --- | --- |
| URUGUAY | September 1, 2004 |
| VENEZUELA | January 1, 1997 |
| YUGOSLAVIA, FEDERAL REPUBLIC OF | December 1, 1991 |
| ZIMBABWE | August 1, 1995 |

SOURCE: U.S. Department of State.

# APPENDIX 15:
# DIRECTORY OF CENTRAL AUTHORITIES

| MEMBER COUNTRY | CENTRAL AUTHORITY | WEBSITE |
|---|---|---|
| ARGENTINA | Ministry of Foreign Affairs | http://www.menores.gov.ar/ |
| AUSTRALIA | Attorney General's Department | http://www.ag.gov.au/ |
| AUSTRIA | Ministry of Justice | http://www.bmj.gv.at/ |
| BAHAMAS | Ministry of Foreign Affairs | www.mfabahamas.org/ |
| BELARUS | Ministry of Justice | http://ncpi.gov.by/minjust/ |
| BELGIUM | Ministry of Justice | http://www.just.fgov.be/ |
| BELIZE | Ministry of Human Development, Women, and Civil Society | http://www.belize.gov.bz/ |
| BRAZIL | Ministry of Justice | http://www.mj.gov.br/ |
| CANADA | Department of Justice | http://www.justice.gouv.qc. ca/ |
| CHILE | Ministry of Justice | http://www.cajmetro.cl/ |
| DENMARK | Ministry of Justice | http://www.boernebortfoerelse.dk/ |
| FINLAND | Ministry of Justice | http://www.om.fi/20726.htm |
| FRANCE | Ministry of Justice | http://www.enlevement-parental.justice.gouv.fr/ |
| GERMANY | Ministry of Justice | http://www.auswaertiges-amt.de/www/en/laenderinfos/konsulat/kindesentziehung.html |
| GREECE | Ministry of Justice | http://www.ministryofjustice.gr/ |
| HUNGARY | Ministry of Justice | http://www.im.hu/ |
| IRELAND | Department of Justice | http://www.justice.ie/ |

| MEMBER COUNTRY | CENTRAL AUTHORITY | WEBSITE |
| --- | --- | --- |
| ISRAEL | Ministry of Justice | http://www.justice.gov.il/ |
| ITALY | Ministry of Justice | http://www.giustizia.it/ |
| MEXICO | Ministry of Foreign Relations | http://www.sre.gob.mx/ |
| NETHERLANDS | Ministry of Justice | http://www.minjus.nl/ |
| NEW ZEALAND | Ministry of Justice | http://www.justice.govt.nz/ |
| NORWAY | Ministry of Justice | http://odin.dep.no/jd/english/bn.html |
| POLAND | Ministry of Justice | http://www.ms.gov.pl/ |
| PORTUGAL | Ministry of Foreign Affairs | http://www.mj.gov.pt/ |
| SOUTH AFRICA | Justice Department | http://www.doj.gov.za/ |
| SPAIN | Ministry of Justice | http://www.justicia.es/ |
| SWEDEN | Ministry of Justice | http://www.sweden.gov.se/ |
| SWITZERLAND | Ministry of Justice | http://www.ejpd.admin.ch/ejpd/de/home.html |
| TURKEY | Ministry of Justice | http://www.adalet.gov.tr/ |
| UNITED KINGDOM (ENGLAND) | Department of Constitutional Affairs | http://www.dca.gov.uk/ |
| UNITED KINGDOM (WALES) | Official Solicitor and Public Trustee | http://www.offsol.demon.co.uk/ |
| UNITED KINGDOM (NORTHERN IRELAND) | Northern Ireland Office | http://www.nio.gov.uk/ |
| UNITED KINGDOM (SCOTLAND) | Justice Department | http://www.scotland.gov.uk/ |
| UNITED STATES OF AMERICA | Department of State | http://www.travel.state.gov/ |

# APPENDIX 16:
# CHILD SUPPORT WORKSHEET

SUPREME COURT OF THE STATE OF NEW YORK
*1* COUNTY OF _____

-----------------------------------------------------------------X

*2*

*3*

                                    Plaintiff,

       -- against --

Index/Docket No.:

CHILD SUPPORT
WORKSHEET

*4*

                                  Defendant

-----------------------------------------------------------------X

*5* Prepared by _____

*6* This Worksheet is submitted by     Plaintiff    Defendant

*(All numbers used in this worksheet are YEARLY figures. Convert weekly or monthly figures to annualized numbers.)*

*7,8* **STEP 1 MANDATORY PARENTAL INCOME** *(b)(5)*          **FATHER**   **MOTHER**

1. Gross (total) income (as reported on most recent Federal tax return, or as computed in accordance with Internal Revenue Code and regulations): *(b)(5)(i)*.......................................................... _____ _____

*The following items **MUST** be added if not already included in Line 1:*

2. Investment income: *(b)(5)(ii)*....................................... _____ _____
3. Workers' compensation: *(b)(5)(iii)(A)*............................. _____ _____
4. Disability benefits: *(b)(5)(iii)(B)*.................................... _____ _____
5. Unemployment insurance benefits: *(b)(5)(iii)(C)*................. _____ _____
6. Social Security benefits: *(b)(5)(iii)(D)*............................. _____ _____
7. Veterans benefits: *(b)(5)(iii)(E)*.................................... _____ _____
8. Pension/retirement income: *(b)(5)(iii)(F)* ........................ _____ _____
9. Fellowships and stipends: *(b)(5)(iii)(G)*............................ _____ _____
10. Annuity payments: *(b)(5)(iii)(H)*.................................. _____ _____
11. If self-employed, depreciation greater than straight-line depreciation used in determining business income or investment credit: *(b)(5)(vi)(A)*.... _____ _____
12. If self-employed, entertainment and travel allowances deducted from business income to the extent the allowances reduce personal expenditures: *(b)(5)(vi)(B)*............................................ _____ _____
13. Former income voluntarily reduced to avoid child support: *(b)(5)(v)*. _____ _____
14. Income voluntarily deferred: *(b)(5)(iii)*............................ _____ _____

**A. TOTAL MANDATORY INCOME:**....................................... _____ _____

(Form UD-8 - Rev. 5/99)

Form reproduced by permission of Author: Steven L. Abel, Esq.

*9, 10* **STEP 2** NON-MANDATORY PARENTAL INCOME

These items must be disclosed here. Their inclusion in the final calculations, however, is discretionary. In contested cases, the Court determines whether or not they are included. In uncontested cases, the parents and their attorneys or mediators must determine which should be included.

15. Income attributable to non-income producing assets: *(b)(5)(iv)(A)*............. _____ _____
16. Employment benefits that confer personal economic benefits: *(b)(5)(iv)(B)*
    (Such as meals, lodging, memberships, automobiles, other)................... _____ _____
    _____ ____ ____
    _____ ____ ____
    _____ ____ ____

17. Fringe benefits of employment: *(b)(5)(iv)(C)*
18. Money, goods and services provided by relatives and friends: *(b)(5)(iv)(D)* _____ _____
    _____ ____ ____
    _____ ____ ____
    _____ ____ ____

  **B. TOTAL NON-MANDATORY INCOME:**.............................................._____

*11, 12*  **C. TOTAL INCOME** *(add Line A + Line B)*:............................._____

*13, 14* **STEP 3** DEDUCTIONS

19. Expenses of investment income listed on line 2: *(b)(5)(ii)*............................ _____ _____
20. Unreimbursed business expenses that do not reduce personal
    expenditures: *(b)(5)(vii)(A)*.............................................................. _____ _____
21. Alimony or maintenance actually paid to a former spouse: *(b)(5)(vii)(B)*...... _____ _____
22. Alimony or maintenance paid to the other parent but only
    if child support will increase when alimony stops: *(b)(5)(vii)(C)*.................. _____ _____
23. Child support actually paid to other children the parent
    is legally obligated to support: *(b)(5)(vii)(D)*.................................................. _____ _____
24. Public assistance: *(b)(5)(vii)(E)*.......................................................... _____ _____
25. Supplemental security income: *(b)(5)(vii)(F)*...................................... _____ _____
26. New York City or Yonkers income or earnings taxes actually paid:
    *(b)(5)(vii)(G)*.......................................................................... _____ _____
27. Social Security taxes (FICA) actually paid: *(b)(5)(vii)(H)*...................................... _____ _____

  **D. TOTAL DEDUCTIONS:**..................................................................._____

*15*    E.   **FATHER'S INCOME** (Line C minus Line D):.................................$

(Form UD-8 - Rev. 5/99)
*16*    F.   **MOTHER'S INCOME** (Line C minus Line D):...........................................$

*17*    **STEP 4** *(b)(4)*   **G. COMBINED PARENTAL INCOME** (Line E + Line F):.......... $

*18*    **STEP 5** *(b)(3) and (c)(2)*

     **MULTIPLY** Line G (up to $80,000) by the proper percentage *(insert in Line H):*
     For 1 child.......................17%    For 3 children..................29%    For 5 or more children.............35% (minimum)
     For 2 children..................25%    For 4 children..................31%

     H.   **COMBINED CHILD SUPPORT:**.......................................................................

     **STEP 6** *(c)(2)*

*19*    DIVIDE the noncustodial parent's amount on Line E or Line F:...........................
*20*    by the amount of Line G:.......................................................................................
     to obtain the percentage allocated
*21*    **I. to the noncustodial parent:**.............................................................................. _____ %

*22*    **STEP 7** *(c)(2)*   **J. MULTIPLY line H by Line I:**...................................

     **STEP 8** *(c)(3)*

*23*    **K. DECIDE** the amount of child support to be paid on any combined
     parental income exceeding $80,000 per year using the percentages
     in STEP 5 or the factors in STEP 11-C or both:...............................................

*24*    **L. ADD** Line J and Line K:.....................................................................................
     This is the amount of child support to be paid by the non-custodial parent to the custodial parent for all costs of the
     children, except for child care expenses, health care expenses, and college, post-secondary, private, special or
     enriched education.

**STEP 9 SPECIAL NUMERICAL FACTORS**

**CHILD CARE EXPENSES**

*25*    M. Cost of child care resulting from custodial parent's
     seeking work *(c)(6)[discretionary]*    working    attending elementary education
     attending secondary education    attending higher education
     attending vocational training leading to employment: *(c)(4)*.......................

*26*    **N. MULTIPLY Line M by Line I:**..................................................................
     This is the amount the non-custodial parent must contribute to the custodial parent

Form reproduced by permission of Author: Steven L. Abel, Esq.

for child care.

(Form UD-8 - Rev. 5/99)

## HEALTH EXPENSES *(c)(5)*

**27**  O.  Reasonable future health care expenses not covered by insurance:........ _____

**28**  P.  MULTIPLY Line O by Line I:................................................................. _____

This is the amount the non-custodial parent must contribute to the custodial parent for health care or pay directly to the health care provider.

**29**  Q.  EDUCATIONAL EXPENSE, if appropriate, see STEP 11(b) *(c)(7)*................ _____

## STEP 10  LOW INCOME EXEMPTIONS *(d)*

**30**  R.  INSERT amount of noncustodial parent's income from Line E or Line F:.. ════════

**31**  S.  ADD amounts on Line L, Line N, Line P and Line Q ▬▬▬▬▬▬
(This total is "basic child support"):.................................................................

**32**  T.  SUBTRACT Line S from Line R:.......................................................................

If Line T is more than the self-support reserve*, then the low income exemptions do not apply and child support remains as determined in Steps 8 and 9. **If so, go to Step 11.**

If Line T is less than the poverty level†, then

**33**  U.  INSERT amount of non-custodial parent's income from Line E or Line F:......... _____

**34**  V.  Self-support reserve:...................................................................................

**35**  W.  SUBTRACT Line V from Line U:..................................................................

If Line W is more than $300 per year, then Line W is the amount of basic child support. If Line W is less than $300 per year, then basic child support must be a minimum of $300 per year.

If Line T is less than the self-support reserve* but more than the poverty level†, then

**36**  X.  INSERT amount of noncustodial parent's income from Line E or Line F:.............. _____

**37**  Y.  Self-support reserve:....................................................................................

*The self-support reserve. This figure changes on April 1 of each year. The current self-support reserve is 135% of the office Federal poverty level for a single person household as promulgated by the U.S. Department of Health and Human Services.

†The poverty level. This figure changes on April 1 of each year. The current Federal poverty level for a single person household in any year is as promulgated by the U.S. Department of Health and Human Services.

**Form reproduced by permission of Author: Steven L. Abel, Esq.**

(Form UD-8 - Rev. 5/99)

38 **Z. SUBTRACT Line Y from Line X**:......................................................................

> If Line Z is more than $600 per year, then Line Z is the amount of basic child support. If Line Z is less than $600 per year, then basic child support must be a minimum of $600 per year.

## STEP 11 NON-NUMERICAL FACTORS

### (a) NON-RECURRING INCOME (e)

> A portion of non-recurring income, such as life insurance proceeds, gifts and inheritances or lottery winnings, may be allocated to child support. The law does not mention a specific percentage for such non-recurring income. Such support is not modified by the low income exemptions.

### (b) EDUCATIONAL EXPENSES (c)(7)

> New York's child support law does not contain a specific percentage method to determine how parents should share the cost of education of their children. Traditionally, the courts have considered both parents' complete financial circumstances in deciding who pays how much. The most important elements of financial circumstances are income, reasonable expenses, and financial resources such as savings and investments.

### (c) ADDITIONAL FACTORS (f)

> The child support guidelines law lists 10 factors that should be considered in deciding on the amount of child support for:
>> combined incomes of more than $80,000 per year or
>> to vary the numerical result of these steps because the result is "unjust or inappropriate". However, any court order deviating from the guidelines must set forth the amount of "basic child support" (Line S) resulting from the Guidelines and the reason for the deviation.

#### These factors are:
1. The financial resources of the parents and the child.
2. The physical and emotional health of the child and his/her special needs and aptitudes.
3. The standard of living the child would have enjoyed if the marriage or household was not dissolved.
4. The tax consequences to the parents.
5. The non-monetary contributions the parents will make toward the care and well-being of the child.
6. The educational needs of the parents.
7. The fact that the gross income of one parent is substantially less than the gross income of the other parent.
8. The needs of the other children of the non-custodial parent for whom the non-custodial parent is providing support, but only (a) if Line 23 is not deducted; (b) after considering the financial resources of any other person obligated to support the other children; and (c) if the resources available to support the other children are less then the resources available to support the children involved in this matter.
9. If a child is not on public assistance, the amount of extraordinary costs of visitation (such as out-of-state travel) or extended visits (other than the usual two to four week summer visits), but only if the custodial parent's expenses are substantially reduced by the visitation involved.
10. Any other factor the court decides is relevant.

(Form UD-8 - Rev. 5/99)

## NON-JUDICIAL DETERMINATION OF CHILD SUPPORT *(h)*

Outside of court, parents are free to agree to any amount of support, so long as they sign a statement that they have been advised of the provisions of the child support guidelines law, the amount of "basic child support" (Line S) resulting from the Guidelines and the reason for any deviation. Further, the Court must approve any deviation, and the court cannot approve agreements of less than $300 per year. This minimum is not per child, meaning that the minimum for 3 children is $300 per year, not $900 per year. In addition, the courts retain discretion over child support.

39

_____

Plaintiff''s Signature

*(The name signed must be printed beneath)*

Subscribed and Sworn to
before me on

_____

_____

NOTARY PUBLIC

Form reproduced by permission of Author: Steven L. Abel, Esq.

# APPENDIX 17:
# QUALIFIED MEDICAL CHILD
# SUPPORT ORDER

At a term of the Supreme Court of the
State of New York, held in and for the
*1* County of_____

*2* at _____, New York

*3* on _____

*4* PRESENT: Hon._____
                    Justice/Referee
------------------------------------------------------------------

*5*
*6*                                                 Index No.:_____
                        Plaintiff,

          -against-                        QUALIFIED MEDICAL
                                           CHILD SUPPORT ORDER
*7*
                        Defendant.
------------------------------------------------------------------

NOTICE: YOUR WILLFUL FAILURE TO OBEY THIS ORDER MAY, AFTER A COURT HEARING, RESULT IN YOUR COMMITMENT TO JAIL FOR A TERM NOT TO EXCEED SIX MONTHS, FOR CONTEMPT OF COURT.

*8* Pursuant to DRL §240(1). This Qualified Medical Child Support Order (QMCSO) orders and directs that the unemancipated dependents named herein:

Name:                Date of Birth:          Soc. Sec.#:          Mailing Address:

are entitled to be enrolled in and receive the benefits for which the legally responsible relative named herein is eligible, under the group health plan named herein in accordance with Section 609 of the Federal Employee Retirement Income Security Act.

*9* The Participant (legally responsible relative) is:
Name:                Soc. Sec.#:             Mailing Address:

*10* The Dependents' Custodial Parent or Legal Guardian who is to be provided with any identification cards and benefit claim forms on behalf of dependents:
Name:                Soc. Sec.#:             Mailing Address:

(Form UD-8b - Rev. 5/99)
*11* The group health plan subject to this order is:

Name:                  Address:                  Identification No.:

*12*  The administrator of said plan is:
      Name:                  Address:

*13*  The type of coverage provided is:

*14*  **ORDERED** that coverage shall include all plans covering the health, medical, dental, pharmaceutical and optical needs of the aforementioned Dependents named above for which the Participant is eligible.

*15*  **ORDERED** that said coverage shall be effective as of (give date) _____
_ and shall continue as available until the respective emancipation of the aforementioned dependents.

**ENTER:**

*16*  DATED:_____              _____
                                                          JSC/Referee

TO:     [Health Insurer]

NOTICE: Pursuant to Section 5241(g)(4) of the Civil Practice Laws and Rules, if an employer, organization or group health plan fails to enroll eligible dependents or to deduct from the debtor's income the debtor's share of the premium, such employer, organization or group health plan administrator shall be jointly and severally liable for all medical expenses incurred on behalf of the debtor's dependents named in the execution while such dependents are not so enrolled to the extent of the insurance benefits that should have been provided under such execution.

The group health plan is not required to provide any type or form of benefit or option not otherwise provided under the group health plan except to the extent necessary to meet the requirements of a law relating to medical child support described in section one thousand three hundred and ninety six g-1 of title forty-two of the United States Code.

(Form UD-8b - Rev. 5/99)

# APPENDIX 18:
# INCOME DEDUCTION ORDER

SUPREME COURT OF THE STATE OF NEW YORK
COUNTY OF _____
-------------------------------------------------------------------x

                                   Plaintiff,           **Index No.** _____

        -against-

                                            INCOME DEDUCTION
                                             ORDER

                                   Defendant.
-------------------------------------------------------------------x

      **ORDERED** that the payments required by the support order issued simultaneously herewith shall be withheld by the debtor's employer from the debtor's compensation, made payable to the creditor identified below and sent to:

                            *Direct Payment*   **OR**      *Forwarded Payment*

                         Address:    _____
                                               _____
                                             _____

Debtor:      Name: _____
                Address: _____
                _____
                Social Security No.:    _____

Creditor:    Name: _____
                Address: _____
                _____
                Social Security No.: _____

Debtor's Employer:          _____
                               _____
                               _____

Amount to be withheld:     $_____ per _____

Date of Termination of Payments: _____

Dated: _____

                              SO ORDERED:

                              _____
                                      Justice

(Appendix - Rev. 5/99)

# APPENDIX 19:
# CHILD PROTECTION PETITION ALLEGING CHILD ABUSE

F.C.A. §§ 1012, 1031

Form 10-7
(Child Protective - Petition--Abuse,
Severe Abuse or Repeated Abuse )
(9/2005)

FAMILY COURT OF NEW YORK
COUNTY OF
..............................................................................

In the Matter of

Docket No.

(A) Child(ren) under Eighteen Years
of Age Alleged to be Abused by

PETITION
❑ Child Abuse
❑ Severe Abuse
❑ Repeated Abuse
[Check applicable box(es)]

Respondent(s)
..............................................................................

**NOTICE:  IF YOUR CHILD IS PLACED IN FOSTER CARE, YOU  MAY LOSE YOUR RIGHTS TO YOUR CHILD AND YOUR CHILD MAY BE ADOPTED WITHOUT YOUR CONSENT.**

**IF YOUR  CHILD STAYS IN FOSTER CARE FOR 15 OF THE MOST RECENT 22 MONTHS, THE  AGENCY MAY BE REQUIRED BY LAW TO FILE A PETITION TO TERMINATE YOUR PARENTAL RIGHTS AND MAY FILE BEFORE THE END OF THE 15-MONTH PERIOD.**

**IF SEVERE OR REPEATED ABUSE IS PROVEN BY  CLEAR AND CONVINCING EVIDENCE, THIS FINDING MAY CONSTITUTE THE BASIS TO TERMINATE YOUR PARENTAL RIGHTS.**

**THE NEXT COURT DATE IS** [specify date]:
**THE PERMANENCY HEARING SHALL BE HELD ON** [specify date]:

TO THE FAMILY COURT:

The undersigned Petitioner respectfully  alleges that

1. Petitioner [specify]:                                        is a [check applicable box]:
   ❑ duly authorized agency having its office and place of business at [specify]:
   ❑ person directed by the Court to originate this proceeding, who  resides at [specify]:

2. The child(ren) who (is) (are) the subject(s) of this proceeding (is)(are):
Name    Sex    Date of Birth    Custodial Parent/Guardian    Child's  Address

---

3. a.  (Upon information and belief) The father and mother of the child(ren) and their respective residence addresses are:

Name of Child(ren)                     Name of Parent                     Parent's Address


b.  (Upon information and belief)  The person(s) legally responsible for the care of the child(ren) (is)(are) [specify]:
who  reside at

4. a.  (Upon information and belief) The child(ren) (is) (are) abused on the following grounds and based upon the following facts [Specify grounds of child abuse  under Family Court Act §1012, as well as supporting facts]:


b.  (Upon information and belief) The following Respondent (s) [specify]:               ,   the
[specify relationship]:                            of the child(ren), (is)(are) the person(s) who
(is)(are) responsible for the abuse of the child(ren).


5. a.  (Upon information and belief (s) The  child(ren) (is) (are) also neglected on the following grounds and based upon the following facts [Specify grounds of child neglect  under Family Court Act §1012, as well as supporting facts]:


b.  (Upon information and belief) The following Respondent (s) [specify]:               ,   the
[specify relationship]:                            of the child(ren), (is)(are) the person(s) who
(is)(are) responsible for the neglect of the child(ren).


6. a.  [Applicable in cases in which severe abuse is alleged]:  (Upon information and belief)
The following Respondent(s) [specify]:                            committed the following act(s)
of severe abuse against the following child(ren) [specify children), act(s), including Penal Law section(s), if applicable, dates, locations, criminal convictions and other facts]:


b. [Applicable in cases in which repeated abuse is alleged](Upon information and belief)
The following  Respondent(s)[specify]:                            committed the following act(s)

of repeated abuse against the following child(ren) [specify child(ren), acts, including Penal Law section(s), if applicable, dates, locations, prior findings of child abuse and other facts]:

    7. [Required if removal has occurred or is requested; check applicable box(es)]:
      a.  ☐ (Upon information and belief) On [specify date]:          , the following child(ren)[specify]:        (was)(were) temporarily removed from the care of the following Respondent(s) [specify]:         on the basis of the following facts and for the following reasons [specify]:
      in accordance with [check applicable box]:
            ☐ a court order pursuant to Family Court Act §1022, issued on [specify]:
            ☐ consent of the following Respondent(s) [specify]:
obtained on [specify date]:        pursuant to Family Court Act §1021.[1]
            ☐ on an emergency basis without a court order pursuant to Family Court Act §1024. There was no time to obtain a court order because [specify]:

      b.  ☐ (Upon information and belief) The child(ren) should be removed from the care of the following Respondent(s) [specify]:        in accordance with Family Court Act §1027 in order to prevent imminent risk to the child(ren)'s life or health on the basis of the following facts and for the following reasons [specify]:

    8. [Required if removal or continued removal of children is requested]:
      a. (Upon information and belief) Continuation in, or return to, the child(ren)'s home would be contrary to the best interests of the child(ren) because [specify facts and reasons]:

      This assertion is based upon the following information [check applicable box(es)]:
        ☐ Report of Suspected Child Abuse or Neglect
        ☐ Case Record, dated [specify]:
        ☐ Service Plan, dated [specify]:
        ☐ The report of [specify]:        , dated [specify]:
        ☐ Other [specify]:

      b. (Upon information and belief) Reasonable efforts, where appropriate, to prevent or eliminate the need for removal of the child(ren) from the home [check applicable box and state reasons as indicated]:

        ☐ were made as follows [specify]:

        ☐ were not made but the lack of efforts was appropriate [check all applicable boxes]:
            ☐ because of a prior judicial finding that the Petitioner was not required to make reasonable efforts to reunify the child(ren) with the

---

[1] A copy of the consent instrument must be attached to the petition. *See* F.C.A. §1021.

Form 10-7   Page 4

Respondent(s) [specify date of finding]:

☐ because [specify other reason(s)]:

☐ were not made.

This assertion is based upon the following information [check applicable box(es)]:
☐ Report of Suspected Child Abuse or Neglect
☐ Case Record, dated [specify]:
☐ Service Plan, dated [specify]:
☐ The report of [specify]:                              , dated [specify]:
☐ Other [specify]:

c. (Upon information and belief)  Based upon Petitioner's  investigation [Check applicable box(es)]: ☐ The following person [specify]:                              is a ☐ non-respondent parent ☐ relative ☐ suitable person  with whom the child(ren) may appropriately reside [specify]:

[Applicable to relatives and other suitable persons]:  Such person:
☐ seeks approval as a foster parent in order to provide care for the child(ren);
☐ wishes to provide care  and custody for the child(ren) without foster care subsidy during  the pendency of any order herein.
☐ may be a resource but not yet determined whether as a foster parent or custodian.

☐ There is no non-respondent parent, relative or suitable person with whom the child(ren) may  appropriately reside.

d. [Required]: (Upon information and belief) Imminent risk to the child(ren)
☐ would  ☐ would not  be eliminated  by the issuance of a temporary order of protection or  order of  protection directing the removal of [specify]:
from the child(ren)'s residence, based upon the following facts and for the following reasons [specify]:

9. The subject child ☐ is ☐ is not  a Native-American child, who is  subject to the Indian Child Welfare Act of 1978 (25 U.S.C. §§ 1901-1963). If so, the following have been notified [check applicable box(es)]:
☐ parent/custodian [specify name and give notification date]:
☐ tribe/nation [specify name and give notification date]:
☐ United States Secretary of the Interior [give notification date]:

10. The  ☐ District Attorney of                  County ☐ Corporation Counsel of the City New York is a party hereto pursuant to section 254(b) of the Family Court Act.

WHEREFORE, Petitioner requests  that an order be made [check applicable box(es)]:
☐ A.  determining the following child(ren)[specify]:                              to be abused by a preponderance of the evidence; and otherwise dealing with the child(ren) in accordance

Form 10-7    Page 5

with the provisions of Article 10 of the Family Court Act;

❑ B.   determining the following child(ren)[specify]:                              to
be ❑ severely  ❑ repeatedly abused  by clear and convincing evidence; and otherwise dealing with
the child(ren) in accordance with the provisions of Article 10 of the Family Court Act;

❑ C.   determining the following child(ren)[specify]:                        to be
neglected by a preponderance of the evidence; and otherwise dealing with the child(ren) in
accordance with the provisions of Article 10 of the Family Court Act;

❑ D.   granting such other and further relief as the Court may deem just and proper.

Dated              ,         .

---

Petitioner

---

Print or Type Name

---

Signature of Attorney, if any

---

Attorney's Name (print or type)

---

Attorney's Address and Telephone Number

VERIFICATION

STATE OF NEW YORK        )
                         )ss.:
COUNTY OF                )
                                   being duly sworn, deposes and says:

That (s)he is
and is acquainted with the facts and circumstances of the above-entitled proceeding; that (s)he has
read the foregoing petition and knows the contents thereof; that the same is true to (his)(her own
knowledge except as to those matters therein stated to be alleged upon information and belief, and
that as to those matters (s)he believes it to be true.

---

Petitioner

Sworn to before me this
        day of

---

(Deputy) (Clerk of the Court)
(Notary Public)

# APPENDIX 20:
# CHILD PROTECTION PETITION ALLEGING
# CHILD NEGLECT

F.C.A. §§ 1012, 1031

Form 10-6
(Child Protective-
Petition -- Neglect)
(9/2005)

FAMILY COURT OF NEW YORK
COUNTY OF
........................................................................................
In the Matter of

      Docket No.

(A) Child(ren) under Eighteen Years          PETITION
of Age Alleged to be Neglected by          (Child Neglect)

            Respondent(s)

........................................................................................

**NOTICE:**   **IF YOUR CHILD IS PLACED IN FOSTER CARE, YOU MAY LOSE YOUR RIGHTS TO YOUR CHILD AND YOUR CHILD MAY BE ADOPTED WITHOUT YOUR CONSENT.**

           **IF YOUR CHILD STAYS IN FOSTER CARE FOR 15 OF THE MOST RECENT 22 MONTHS, THE AGENCY MAY BE REQUIRED BY LAW TO FILE A PETITION TO TERMINATE YOUR PARENTAL RIGHTS AND MAY FILE BEFORE THE END OF THE 15-MONTH PERIOD.**

           TO THE FAMILY COURT:
           The undersigned Petitioner respectfully alleges that:

           1. Petitioner [specify]:          is a [check applicable box]:
           ❑ duly authorized agency having its office and place of business at [specify]:
           ❑ person directed by the Court to originate this proceeding, who resides at
           [specify]:

           2. The child(ren) who (is) (are) the subject(s) of this proceeding (is)(are):
Name     Sex    Date of Birth    Custodial Parent/Guardian    Child's Address

b.  (Upon information and belief)  The person(s) legally responsible for the care of said child(ren) (is)(are)[specify]:

who reside at [specify address]:

4.  (Upon information and belief) The child(ren) (is) (are) a(n) neglected on the following grounds and based upon the following facts [Specify grounds of child neglect under Family Court Act §1012, as well as supporting facts]:

5.  (Upon information and belief), Respondent(s) [specify]:
, the { specify relationship]:
of the child(ren), (is)(are) the person(s) who (is)(are) responsible for the neglect of the child(ren).

6. [Required if removal has occurred or is requested; check applicable box(es)]:
a.  ☐ (Upon information and belief) On [specify date]:                , the following child(ren)[specify]:                were temporarily removed from the care of the following Respondent(s) [specify]:                on the basis of the following facts and for the following reasons [specify]:

in accordance with [check applicable box]:
☐ a court order pursuant to Family Court Act §1022, issued on [specify]:
☐ consent of the following Respondent(s) [specify]:
obtained on [specify date]:                pursuant to Family Court Act §1021.[1]
☐ on an emergency basis without a court order pursuant to Family Court Act §1024.  There was no time to obtain a court order because [specify]:

b.  ☐ (Upon information and belief)  The child(ren) should be removed from the care of the following Respondent(s) [specify]:                in accordance with Family Court Act §1027  in order to prevent imminent risk to the child(ren)'s life or health on the basis of the following facts and for the following reasons [specify]:

7. [Required if removal or continued removal of children is requested]:
a.  (Upon information and belief) Continuation in, or return to, the child(ren)'s home would be contrary to the best interests of the child(ren) because [specify facts and reasons]:

This assertion is based upon the following information [check applicable box(es)]:
☐ Report of Suspected Child Abuse or Neglect
☐ Case Record, dated [specify]:

---

[1] A copy of the consent instrument must be attached to the petition. *See* F.C.A. §1021.

☐ Service Plan, dated [specify]:
☐ The report of [specify]:                                      , dated [specify]:
☐ Other [specify]:

      b.  (Upon information and belief) Reasonable efforts, where appropriate, to prevent or eliminate the need for removal of the child(ren) from the home [check applicable box and state reasons as indicated]:

    ☐  were made as follows [specify]:

    ☐  were not made but the lack of efforts was appropriate [check all applicable boxes]:
        ☐ because of a prior judicial finding that the Petitioner was not required to make reasonable efforts to reunify the child(ren) with the Respondent(s) [specify date of finding]:

        ☐ because [specify other reason(s)]:

☐ were not made.

This assertion is based upon the following information [check applicable box(es)]:
    ☐ Report of Suspected Child Abuse or Neglect
    ☐ Case Record, dated [specify]:
    ☐ Service Plan, dated [specify]:
    ☐ The report of [specify]:                                      , dated [specify]:
    ☐ Other [specify]:

      c.  (Upon information and belief) Based upon Petitioner's investigation [Check applicable box(es)]:

    ☐ The following person [specify]:
is a ☐ non-respondent parent ☐ relative ☐ suitable person with whom the child(ren) may appropriately reside.
    [Applicable to relatives and other suitable persons]:  Such person:
    ☐ seeks approval as a foster parent in order to provide care for the child(ren);
    ☐ wishes to provide care and custody for the child(ren) without foster care
      subsidy during the pendency of any order herein.
    ☐ may be a resource but not yet determined whether as a foster parent or custodian.

    ☐ There is no non-respondent parent, relative or suitable person with whom the child(ren) may appropriately reside.

      d.  (Upon information and belief) Imminent risk to the child(ren) ☐ would ☐ would not be eliminated by the issuance of a temporary order of protection or order of protection directing the removal of [specify]:                                from the child(ren)'s residence, based upon the following facts and for the following reasons [specify]:

Form 10-6   Page 4

8. The subject child ❑ is ❑ is not a Native-American child, who is subject to the Indian Child Welfare Act of 1978 (25 U.S.C. §§ 1901-1963). If so, the following have been notified [check applicable box(es)]:

❑ parent/custodian [specify name and give notification date]:

❑ tribe/nation [specify name and give notification date]:

❑ United States Secretary of the Interior [give notification date]:

WHEREFORE, Petitioner requests that an order be issued determining the child(ren) to be neglected and otherwise dealing with the child(ren) in accordance with the provisions of Article 10 of the Family Court Act.

Dated                 ,             .

_____
Petitioner

_____
Print or Type Name

_____
Signature of Attorney, if any

_____
Attorney's Name (print or type)

_____
_____
_____
Attorney's Address and Telephone Number

VERIFICATION

STATE OF NEW YORK        )
                                            )ss.:
COUNTY OF                      )

_____ being duly sworn, deposes and says:
That (s)he is

and is acquainted with the facts and circumstances of the above-entitled proceeding; that (s)he has read the foregoing petition and knows the contents thereof; that the same is true to (his)(her own knowledge except as to those matters therein stated to be alleged upon information and belief, and that as to those matters (s)he believes it to be true.

_____
Petitioner

Sworn to before me this
          day of

_____
(Deputy) (Clerk of the Court)
(Notary Public)

# APPENDIX 21:
# PATERNITY PETITION

F. C. A. §§ 522, 523                                        Form 5-1
S.S.L. §111-g                                               (Paternity)
                                                            (9/2005)

FAMILY COURT OF THE STATE OF NEW YORK
COUNTY OF
.......................................................................................

In the Matter of a Paternity Proceeding                    Docket No.

                                    Petitioner,            PATERNITY
S.S.#                                                       PETITION
              -against-                                     (Parent)

                                    Respondent
S.S.#
.......................................................................................

TO THE FAMILY COURT:

The undersigned petitioner respectfully shows that:

1.  a. Petitioner resides at

    b. Respondent resides at


2.  Petitioner had sexual intercourse with the above-named Respondent during a period of
time beginning on or about the        day of                  ,      , and ending on or about
the      day of              ,      , and as a result thereof (Petitioner) (Respondent) became
pregnant.

[Alternative allegations; delete inapplicable provisions]:

3.  (a) (Petitioner) (Respondent) gave birth to a (male) (female) child out of wedlock on the
        day of

    (b) (Petitioner) (Respondent) is now pregnant with a child who is likely to be born out of
wedlock.

4.  (Petitioner) (Respondent) is the father of the child

5.  At the time of conception of the child, the mother
(was not married).
(was married to [name]                                   whose last known address is
                                                                            ).

Form 5-1 page 2

6. (Petitioner) (Respondent) (has acknowledged) (acknowledges) paternity of the child (in writing) (and) (by furnishing support).

7. The name, date of birth and social security number of the child involved is:

| Name | Date of birth | Social Security # |
|------|---------------|-------------------|

8. No previous application has been made to any court or judge for the relief herein requested (except [specify]:

).

9. Petitioner: [alternative allegations, delete inapplicable clauses]

(a: has made application for child support services with the local Department of Social Services).

(b: hereby makes application for child support enforcement services by the filing of this petition).

(c: does not wish to make application for child support services).

(d: is the non-custodial parent of the subject child).

10. The subject child (is)(is not) a Native American child subject to the Indian Child Welfare Act of 1978 (25 U.S.C. §§ 1901-1963).

11. Pursuant to F.C.A §§ 545, upon the entry of an Order of Filiation, the Court shall, upon application of either party, enter an order of support for the subject child.

WHEREFORE, Petitioner requests that this Court issue a summons or warrant requiring the Respondent to show cause why the Court should not enter a declaration of paternity, an order of support and such other and further relief as may be appropriate under the circumstances.

NOTE: (1) A COURT ORDER OF SUPPORT RESULTING FROM A PROCEEDING COMMENCED BY THIS APPLICATION (PETITION) SHALL BE ADJUSTED BY THE APPLICATION OF A COST OF LIVING ADJUSTMENT AT THE DIRECTION OF THE SUPPORT COLLECTION UNIT NO EARLIER THAN TWENTY-FOUR MONTHS AFTER SUCH ORDER IS ISSUED, LAST MODIFIED OR LAST

ADJUSTED, UPON THE REQUEST OF ANY PARTY TO THE ORDER OR PURSUANT TO PARAGRAPH (2) BELOW. SUCH COST OF LIVING ADJUSTMENT SHALL BE ON NOTICE TO BOTH PARTIES WHO, IF THEY OBJECT TO THE COST OF LIVING ADJUSTMENT, SHALL HAVE THE RIGHT TO BE HEARD BY THE COURT AND TO PRESENT EVIDENCE WHICH THE COURT WILL CONSIDER IN ADJUSTING THE CHILD SUPPORT ORDER IN ACCORDANCE WITH SECTION FOUR HUNDRED THIRTEEN OF THE FAMILY COURT ACT, KNOWN AS THE CHILD SUPPORT STANDARDS ACT.

(2) A PARTY SEEKING SUPPORT FOR ANY CHILD(REN) RECEIVING FAMILY ASSISTANCE SHALL HAVE A CHILD SUPPORT ORDER REVIEWED AND ADJUSTED AT THE DIRECTION OF THE SUPPORT COLLECTION UNIT NO EARLIER THAN TWENTY-FOUR MONTHS AFTER SUCH ORDER IS ISSUED, LAST MODIFIED OR LAST ADJUSTED BY THE SUPPORT COLLECTION UNIT, WITHOUT FURTHER APPLICATION BY ANY PARTY. ALL PARTIES WILL RECEIVE A COPY OF THE ADJUSTED ORDER.

(3) WHERE ANY PARTY FAILS TO PROVIDE, AND UPDATE UPON ANY CHANGE, THE SUPPORT COLLECTION UNIT WITH A CURRENT ADDRESS, AS REQUIRED BY SECTION FOUR HUNDRED FORTY-THREE OF THE FAMILY COURT ACT, TO WHICH AN ADJUSTED ORDER CAN BE SENT, THE SUPPORT OBLIGATION AMOUNT CONTAINED THEREIN SHALL BECOME DUE AND OWING ON THE DATE THE FIRST PAYMENT IS DUE UNDER THE TERMS OF THE ORDER OF SUPPORT WHICH WAS REVIEWED AND ADJUSTED OCCURRING ON OR AFTER THE EFFECTIVE DATE OF THE ADJUSTED ORDER, REGARDLESS OF WHETHER OR NOT THE PARTY HAS RECEIVED A COPY OF THE ADJUSTED ORDER.

_____
Petitioner
_____
Print or type name

_____
Signature of Attorney, if any

_____
Attorney's Name (Print or Type)

_____
_____
_____
Attorney's Address and Telephone Number

Dated:           ,     .

Form 5-1 page 4

VERIFICATION

STATE OF NEW YORK )
                     : ss.:
COUNTY OF         )

being duly sworn, says that (s)he is the Petitioner in the above-entitled proceeding and that the foregoing petition is true to (his)(her) own knowledge, except as to matters herein stated to be alleged on information and belief and as to those matters (s)he believes it to be true.

_____
                           Petitioner

Sworn to before me this
      day of     ,  .

_____
(Deputy) Clerk of the Court
    Notary Public

# APPENDIX 22:
# ORDER OF FILIATION AND SUPPORT

F.C.A. §§ 413, 418, 440, 532,
536, 542, 545, 571; Art.5-B

Form 5-8
(Order of Filiation and
Support)
7/2003

At a term of the Family Court of the
State of New York held in and for the
County of              ,
at            New York
on

PRESENT Hon. _____
              Judge/Support Magistrate

......................................................................................

In the Matter of a Paternity Proceeding

(Commissioner of Social Services, Assignee,
on behalf of               , Assignor)

                       Petitioner,

S.S.# (Assignor)

        -against-

                    Respondent

S.S.#

......................................................................................

Docket No.

ORDER OF
FILIATION AND
SUPPORT

**NOTICE:** YOUR WILLFUL FAILURE TO OBEY THIS ORDER MAY RESULT IN INCARCERATION FOR CRIMINAL NON-SUPPORT OR CONTEMPT; SUSPENSION OF YOUR DRIVER'S LICENSE, STATE-ISSUED PROFESSIONAL, TRADE, BUSINESS AND OCCUPATIONAL LICENSES AND RECREATIONAL AND SPORTING LICENSES AND PERMITS; AND IMPOSITION OF REAL OR PERSONAL PROPERTY LIENS.

**IF THIS ORDER IS ENTERED BY A JUDGE,** PURSUANT TO SECTION 1113 OF THE FAMILY COURT ACT, AN APPEAL FROM THIS ORDER MUST BE TAKEN WITHIN 30 DAYS OF RECEIPT OF THE ORDER BY APPELLANT IN COURT, OR 30 DAYS AFTER SERVICE BY A PARTY OR THE LAW GUARDIAN UPON THE APPELLANT, OR 35 DAYS FROM THE DATE OF MAILING OF THE ORDER TO APPELLANT BY THE CLERK OF COURT, WHICHEVER IS EARLIEST.

**IF THIS ORDER IS ENTERED BY A SUPPORT MAGISTRATE,** SPECIFIC WRITTEN OBJECTIONS TO THIS ORDER MAY BE FILED WITH THIS COURT WITHIN 30 DAYS OF THE DATE THE ORDER WAS RECEIVED IN COURT OR BY PERSONAL SERVICE, OR IF THE ORDER WAS RECEIVED BY MAIL, WITHIN 35 DAYS OF THE MAILING OF THE ORDER.

Form 5-8 Page 2

The above-named Petitioner having filed a petition, sworn to                    ,          ,
alleging that the above-named                    □ Petitioner □ Respondent is the father of a
□ male □ female child □ born □ about to be born out of wedlock to
on          ,          , and that □ the mother and/or child is or is likely to become a public charge; and

The Respondent having □ appeared □ been brought before this Court to show cause why a
declaration of paternity, order of support and other relief prayed for in the petition should not be made;
and the Respondent having □ denied □ admitted the allegations of the petition; and

The matter having duly come on to be heard before this Court;

NOW, after examination and inquiry into the facts and circumstances of the case and after
hearing the proofs and testimony offered in relation thereto, it is

ADJUDGED and DECLARED that the above-named □ Petitioner □ Respondent is the
father of the child; and the Court finds that:

The basic child support obligation is $            □ weekly □ every two weeks □ monthly
□twice per month □ quarterly   for support of the following child(ren):
NAME                                        DATE OF BIRTH   SOCIAL SECURITY #

The mother is the □ custodial □ non-custodial parent, whose pro rata share of the basic child
support obligation is  $            □ weekly □ every two weeks □ monthly □twice per month   □
quarterly.

The father is the □ custodial □ non-custodial parent, whose pro rata share of the basic child
obligation is $            □ weekly □ every two weeks □ monthly □twice per month   □ quarterly.
                                                                                                    ;

And the Court finds further that:

□ The non-custodial parent's pro rata share of the basic child support obligation is neither
unjust nor inappropriate; [1]
                                    OR
□ Upon consideration of the following factors specified in Family Court Act §
413(1)(f)[specify factors]:

the non-custodial parent's pro rata share of the basic child support obligation is  □ unjust
□ inappropriate for the following reasons [specify]:[2]

[Applicable in cases in which the parties stipulated to an order of child support]:
□ The parties have voluntarily stipulated to child support for the child(ren) [names]:
payable by [specify]:_____ in the amount of $_____ □ weekly
□ every two weeks □ monthly □twice per month □ quarterly.

---

[1] This paragraph is to be used if the basic child support obligation is applied without
deviation.

[2] This paragraph is to be used if the court's order deviates from the basic child support
obligation, pursuant to F.C.A. § 413(1)(g).

Form 5-8 page 3

☐ This stipulation has been entered into the record and recites, in compliance with Section 413(1)(h) of the Family Court Act, that [check applicable box(es)]:

a. The parties have been advised of the provisions of Section 413(1)of the Family Court Act;

b. The unrepresented party, if any, has received a copy of the child support standards chart promulgated by the Commissioner of the N.Y.S. Office of Temporary and Disability Assistance pursuant to Section 111-i of the Social Services Law;

c. The basic child support obligation as defined in Family Court Act Section 413(1) presumptively results in the correct amount of child support to be awarded;

d. The basic child support obligation in this case is $_____ ☐ weekly ☐ every two weeks ☐ monthly ☐twice per month ☐ quarterly; and

e. The parties' reason(s) for agreeing to child support in an amount different from the basic child support obligation (is) (are) [specify]:
                                                                                                    ;

☐ The Court approves the parties' agreement to deviate from the basic child support obligation for the following reasons: [specify; see Family Court Act § 413(1)(f)]:

The name, address and telephone number of Respondent's current employer(s) are:

NAME                              ADDRESS                        TELEPHONE

NOW, therefore, it is [check applicable box(es)]:

☐ ORDERED that the above-named ☐ Petitioner ☐ Respondent, upon notice of this order, pay or cause to be paid to                                                        ☐ as Trustee ☐ IV-D cases: Support Collection Unit ☐ Non-IV-D cases: N.Y.S. Office of Temporary and Disability Assistance,[4] the sum of $_____ ☐ weekly ☐ every two weeks ☐ monthly ☐twice per month ☐ quarterly commencing [specify date]:                                     , for the support and education of the child until the child reaches the age of twenty-one years; and it is further

☐ ORDERED that the ☐ Petitioner ☐ Respondent pay or cause to be paid to
                          ☐ as Trustee ☐ IV-D cases: Support Collection Unit ☐ Non-IV-D cases: NYS Office of Temporary and Disability Assistance),[5] the sum of $             which amount represents reimbursement for the needs of the child accruing from the date of the birth of the child to the date of the application for this order, which sum may be paid at the rate of $       weekly ☐ every two weeks ☐ monthly ☐twice per month ☐ quarterly       until the sum of $ is fully paid; and it is further

[4]Non-IV-D cases only: payments must be remitted to: N.Y.S. Office of Temporary and Disability Assistance, P.O. Box 15365, Albany, New York 12260

[5]Non-IV-D cases only: payments must be remitted to: N.Y.S. Office of Temporary and Disability Assistance, P.O. Box 15365, Albany, New York 12260

Form 5-8 page 4

□ ORDERED that the □ Petitioner □ Respondent pay or cause to be paid to
□ as Trustee, □ IV-D cases: Support Collection Unit, □ Non-IV-D cases:
N.Y.S. Office of Temporary and Disability Assistance),[6] the sum of $    as and for the necessary
expenses incurred or to be incurred by or for the mother in connection with her pregnancy,
confinement and recovery, which sum may be paid at the rate of $    □ weekly □ every two
weeks □ monthly □twice per month □ quarterly commencing on    ,    ,
until the sum of $    is fully paid; and it is further

[Non-IV-D cases only]: □ ORDERED that, pursuant to Family Court Act Section
440(1)(b)(2), this order shall be enforceable by immediate income deduction order issued in
accordance with Section 5242 of the Civil Practice Law and Rules; and it is further

□ ORDERED that, for the following reason(s)

constituting good cause pursuant to Section 440(1)(b) of the Family Court Act, the □ IV-D cases:
Support Collection Unit □ Non-IV-D cases: Court    shall NOT issue an immediate income
execution; however, in the event of default,[7] this order shall be enforceable pursuant to Section 5241
or 5242 of the Civil Practice Law and Rules, or in any other manner provided by law; and it is further

[IV-D cases only]: □ ORDERED that the Respondent, custodial parent and any other
individual parties immediately notify the Support Collection Unit of any changes in the following
information: residential and mailing addresses, social security number, telephone number, driver's
license number; and name, address and telephone numbers of the parties' employers and of any change
in health insurance benefits, including any termination of benefits, change in the health insurance
benefit carrier or premium, or extent and availability of existing or new benefits;

And the Court having determined that [check applicable box]:
□ The child(ren) are currently covered by the following health insurance plan [specify]:
which is maintained by [specify party]:

□ Health insurance coverage would be available to one of the parents or a legally-responsible relative
[specify name]:    under the following health insurance plan [specify, if known]:
which provides the following health insurance benefits [specify extent and type of benefits, if
known, including any medical, dental, optical, prescription drug and health care services or other
health care benefits]:

□ Health insurance coverage is available to both of the parents as follows:
    Name    Health Insurance Plan    Premium or Contribution    Benefits

---

[6]Non-IV-D cases only: payments must be remitted to: N.Y.S. Office of Temporary and
Disability Assistance, P.O. Box 15365, Albany, New York

[7]"Default", as defined in CPLR §5241, means the failure to remit three payments on the
date due in the full amount directed in this order, or the accumulation of arrears, including
amounts arising from retroactive support, that are equal to or greater than the amount directed to
be paid for one month, whichever occurs first.

Form 5-8 page 5

☐ No legally-responsible relative has health insurance coverage available for the child(ren), but the child(ren)      may be eligible for health insurance benefits under the New York "Child Health Plus   program or the New York State Medical Assistance Program,

IT IS THEREFORE ORDERED that [specify name(s) of legally-responsible relative(s)]:

☐ continue to maintain health insurance coverage for the following eligible dependent(s)
[specify]:                        under the above-named existing plan for as long as it remains available;
☐ enroll the following eligible dependent(s) [specify]:
under the following health insurance plan [specify]:                                    immediately
and without regard to seasonal enrollment restrictions, effective as of [specify date]:
, and maintain such coverage as long as it remains available in accordance with
[IV-D cases]: ☐ the Medical Execution, which shall be issued immediately by
the Support Collection Unit, pursuant to CPLR 5241
☐ the Medical Execution issued by this Court
[Non-IV-D cases]: ☐ the Qualified Medical Child Support Order.

SUCH COVERAGE SHALL INCLUDE ALL PLANS COVERING THE HEALTH, MEDICAL, DENTAL, OPTICAL AND PRESCRIPTION DRUG NEEDS OF THE DEPENDENTS NAMED ABOVE AND ANY OTHER HEALTH CARE SERVICES OR BENEFITS FOR WHICH THE LEGALLY-RESPONSIBLE RELATIVE IS ELIGIBLE FOR THE BENEFIT OF SUCH DEPENDENTS; PROVIDED, HOWEVER, THAT THE GROUP HEALTH PLAN IS NOT REQUIRED TO PROVIDE ANY TYPE OR FORM OF BENEFIT OR OPTION NOT OTHERWISE PROVIDED UNDER THE GROUP HEALTH PLAN EXCEPT TO THE EXTENT NECESSARY TO MEET THE REQUIREMENTS OF SECTION 1396(G-1) OF TITLE 42 OF THE UNITED STATES CODE. THE LEGALLY-RESPONSIBLE RELATIVE(S) SHALL ASSIGN ALL INSURANCE REIMBURSEMENT PAYMENTS FOR HEALTH CARE EXPENSES INCURRED FOR (HIS)(HER) ELIGIBLE DEPENDENT(S) TO THE PROVIDER OF SUCH SERVICES OR THE PARTY HAVING ACTUALLY INCURRED AND SATISFIED SUCH EXPENSES, AS APPROPRIATE;

OR

☐ This Court having found that neither of the parties have health insurance coverage available to cover the child(ren), it is hereby
ORDERED that the custodial parent [specify name]:
shall immediately apply to enroll the eligible child(ren) in the "Child Health Plus   program (the NYS health insurance program for children) and the New York State Medical Assistance Program.

And the Court further finds that:

The mother is the ☐ custodial ☐ non-custodial parent, whose pro rata share of the cost or premiums to obtain or maintain such health insurance coverage is _____;
The father is the ☐ custodial ☐ non-custodial parent, whose pro rata share of the cost or premiums to obtain or maintain such health insurance coverage is _____;

And the Court further finds that [check applicable box]:

☐ Each parent shall pay the cost of the premiums or family contribution in the same proportion as each of their incomes are to the combined parental income as follows[ specify]:

☐ Upon consideration of the following factors [specify]:

pro-rating the payment would be unjust or inappropriate for the following reasons [specify]:

Therefore, the payments shall be allocated as follows [specify]:

Form 5-8 page 6

; and it is further
ORDERED that the legally responsible relative immediately notify the [check applicable box]: ☐ other party (non-IV-D cases)  ☐ Support Collection Unit (IV-D cases) of any change in health insurance benefits, including any termination of benefits, change in the health insurance benefit carrier or premium, or extent and availability of existing or new benefits; and it is further

ORDERED that [specify name]:                    shall execute and deliver to [specify name]:                    any forms, notices, documents, or instruments to assure timely payment of any health insurance claims for said dependent(s); and it is further

ORDERED that upon a finding that the above-named legally-responsible relative(s) willfully failed to obtain health insurance benefits in violation of [check applicable box(es)]: ☐ this order
☐ the medical execution  ☐ the qualified medical child support order, such relative(s) will be presumptively liable for all health care expenses incurred on behalf of the above-named defendant(s) from the first date such dependent(s) ☐ was ☐were eligible to be enrolled to receive health insurance benefits after the issuance of such order or execution directing the acquisition of such coverage; and it is further

ORDERED that [specify]:                    the legally-responsible relative(s) herein, shall pay ☐ his ☐ her pro rata share of future reasonable health expenses of the child(ren) not covered by insurance by [check applicable box]: ☐ direct payments to the health care provider ☐ other [specify]:
; and it is further

ORDERED that, if health insurance benefits for the above-named child(ren) not available at the present time become available in the future to the legally-responsible relative(s), such relative(s) shall enroll the dependent(s) who are eligible for such benefits immediately and without regard to seasonal enrollment restrictions and shall maintain such benefits so long as they remain available; and it is further

[Check applicable box(es):
        ☐ ORDERED that                    , the non-custodial parent herein, pay the sum of $            as ☐ his ☐ her proportionate share of reasonable child care expenses, to be paid as follows:

; and it is further

        ☐ ORDERED that                    , the non-custodial parent herein, pay the sum of $            as educational expenses by ☐ direct payment to the educational provider ☐ other [specify]:
; and it is further

        ☐ ORDERED that [specify party or parties; check applicable box(es):
☐        purchase and maintain ☐ life  and/or  ☐ accident insurance policy in the
        amount of [specify]: _____ and/or
☐        maintain the following existing ☐ life  and/or  ☐ accident insurance policy in the
        amount of [specify]: _____ and/or
☐        assign the following as ☐ beneficiary ☐ beneficiaries [specify]: _____
        to the following existing ☐ life  and/or  ☐ accident insurance policy or policies
        [specify policy or policies and amount(s)]: _____.

Form 5-8 page 7

In the case of life insurance, the following shall be designated as irrevocable beneficiaries [specify]: _____ during the following time period [specify]: _____.

In the case of accident insurance, the insured party shall be designated as irrevocable beneficiary during the following time period [specify]: _____.

The obligation to provide such insurance shall cease upon the termination of the duty of [specify party]: _____ to provide support for each child;. and it is further

[IV-D Cases}: □ ORDERED that when the person or family to whom family assistance is being paid, no longer receives family assistance, support payments shall continue to be made to the Support Collection Unit, unless such person or family requests otherwise;) and it is further

□ ORDERED that Respondent shall have the following rights of visitation with respect to the child(ren)[specify]:[8]

**[REQUIRED]** IT IS FURTHER ORDERED that a copy of this order be provided promptly by [check applicable box]:□ Support Collection Unit ((IV-D cases: ) □ Clerk of Court (non-IV-D cases) to the New York State Case Registry of Child Support Orders established pursuant to Section 111-b(4-a) of the Social Services Law; and it is further

ORDERED that [specify]:

NOTE: (1) THIS ORDER OF CHILD SUPPORT SHALL BE ADJUSTED BY THE APPLICATION OF A COST OF LIVING ADJUSTMENT AT THE DIRECTION OF THE SUPPORT COLLECTION UNIT NO EARLIER THAN TWENTY-FOUR MONTHS AFTER THIS ORDER IS ISSUED, LAST MODIFIED OR LAST ADJUSTED, UPON THE REQUEST OF ANY PARTY TO THE ORDER OR PURSUANT TO PARAGRAPH ( 2) BELOW. UPON APPLICATION OF A COST OF LIVING ADJUSTMENT AT THE DIRECTION OF THE SUPPORT COLLECTION UNIT, AN ADJUSTED ORDER SHALL BE SENT TO THE PARTIES WHO, IF THEY OBJECT TO THE COST OF LIVING ADJUSTMENT, SHALL HAVE THIRTY-FIVE (35) DAYS FROM THE DATE OF MAILING TO SUBMIT A WRITTEN OBJECTION TO THE COURT INDICATED ON SUCH ADJUSTED ORDER. UPON RECEIPT OF SUCH WRITTEN OBJECTION, THE COURT SHALL SCHEDULE A HEARING AT WHICH THE PARTIES MAY BE PRESENT TO OFFER EVIDENCE WHICH THE COURT WILL CONSIDER IN ADJUSTING THE CHILD SUPPORT ORDER IN ACCORDANCE WITH THE CHILD SUPPORT STANDARDS ACT. (2) A RECIPIENT OF FAMILY ASSISTANCE SHALL HAVE THE CHILD SUPPORT ORDER REVIEWED AND ADJUSTED AT THE DIRECTION OF THE SUPPORT COLLECTION UNIT NO EARLIER THAN TWENTY-FOUR MONTHS AFTER SUCH ORDER IS ISSUED, LAST MODIFIED OR LAST ADJUSTED WITHOUT FURTHER APPLICATION OF ANY PARTY. ALL PARTIES WILL RECEIVE NOTICE OF ADJUSTMENT FINDINGS.

(3) WHERE ANY PARTY FAILS TO PROVIDE, AND UPDATE UPON ANY CHANGE, THE SUPPORT COLLECTION UNIT WITH A CURRENT ADDRESS, AS REQUIRED BY SECTION FOUR HUNDRED FORTY-THREE OF THE FAMILY COURT ACT, TO WHICH AN ADJUSTED ORDER CAN BE SENT, THE SUPPORT OBLIGATION AMOUNT CONTAINED THEREIN SHALL BECOME DUE AND OWING ON THE DATE THE

---

[8] Judicial orders only.

Form 5-8 page 8

FIRST             PAYMENT IS DUE UNDER THE TERMS OF THE ORDER OF
SUPPORT                                        WHICH WAS REVIEWED
AND ADJUSTED
OCCURRING ON OR
AFTER THE EFFECTIVE
DATE OF THE ORDER,
REGARDLESS OF
WHETHER OR NOT THE
PARTY HAS RECEIVED A
COPY OF THE ADJUSTED
ORDER.

ENTER

JUDGE OF THE FAMILY COURT/SUPPORT MAGISTRATE

DATED: _____ , _____ .
CHECK APPLICABLE BOX:
□ ORDER MAILED ON [SPECIFY DATE(S) AND TO WHOM MAILED ]: _____
□ ORDER RECEIVED IN COURT ON [SPECIFY DATE(S) AND TO WHOM GIVEN]: _____

# GLOSSARY

**Abandonment**—A ground for divorce. Abandonment occurs when the Defendant has willfully left the Plaintiff continuously, usually for a period of one year or more, without the plaintiff's consent.

**Abduction**—The criminal or tortious act of taking and carrying away by force.

**Abscond**—To secrete oneself from the jurisdiction of the courts.

**Acquiescence**—Conduct that may imply consent.

**Action at Law**—A judicial proceeding whereby one party prosecutes another for a wrong done.

**Actionable**—Giving rise to a cause of action.

**Adjudication**—The determination of a controversy and pronouncement of judgment.

**Adjudicatory Hearing**—The process by which it is determined whether the allegations in a complaint can be proven and, if so, whether they fall within the jurisdictional categories of the juvenile court.

**Admissible Evidence**—Evidence which may be received by a trial court to assist the trier of fact, either the judge or jury, in deciding a dispute.

**Adoption**—Legal process pursuant to state statute in which a child's legal rights and duties toward his natural parent(s) are terminated, and similar rights and duties toward his adoptive parents are substituted.

**Adultery**—A ground for divorce. Adultery is any sexual act or deviate sexual act with a partner other than the spouse.

**Adversary**—Opponent or litigant in a legal controversy or litigation.

**Adversary Proceeding**—A proceeding involving a real controversy contested by two opposing parties.

**Affidavit of Service**—An oath that litigation papers were properly served upon the opposing party.

**Ancillary Relief**—Additional or supplemental relief sought in a divorce action, such as custody, child support, etc.

**Annulment**—To make void by competent authority.

**Answer**—In a civil proceeding, the principal pleading on the part of the defendant in response to the plaintiff's complaint.

**Appeal**—Resort to a higher court for the purpose of obtaining a review of a lower court decision.

**Appearance**—To come into court, personally or through an attorney, after being summoned.

**Appellate Court**—A court having jurisdiction to review the law as applied to a prior determination of the same case.

**Argument**—A discourse set forth for the purpose of establishing one's position in a controversy.

**Arrears**—Money which is overdue and unpaid.

**Bench**—The court and the judges composing the court collectively.

**Burden of Proof**—The duty of a party to substantiate an allegation or issue to convince the trier of fact as to the truth of their claim.

**Caption**—The heading of a legal document which contains the name of the court, the index number assigned to the matter, and the names of the parties.

**Cause of Action**—The factual basis for bringing a lawsuit.

**Certiorari**—A common law writ whereby a higher court requests a review of a lower court's records to determine whether any irregularities occurred in a particular proceeding.

**Child Abuse**—Any form of cruelty to a child's physical, moral or mental well-being.

**Child Custody**—The care, control and maintenance of a child which may be awarded by a court to one of the parents of the child.

**Child Labor Laws**—Network of laws on both federal and state levels, prescribing working conditions for children in terms of hours and nature of work which may be performed, all designed to protect the child.

**Child Protective Agency**—A state agency responsible for the investigation of child abuse and neglect reports.

**Child Support**—The legal obligation of parents to contribute to the economic maintenance of their children.

**Child Welfare**—A generic term which embraces the totality of measures necessary for a child's well being; physical, moral and mental.

**Circumstantial Evidence**—Indirect evidence by which a principal fact may be inferred.

**Civil Action**—An action maintained to protect a private, civil right as opposed to a criminal action.

**Civil Court**—The court designed to resolve disputes arising under the common law and civil statutes.

**Civil Law**—Law which applies to noncriminal actions.

**Claimant**—The party who brings the arbitration petition, also known as the plaintiff.

**Clean Hands Doctrine**—The concept that claimants who seek equitable relief must not themselves have indulged in any impropriety in relation to the transaction upon which relief is sought.

**Cohabit**—To live together as husband and wife.

**Cohabitation**—The mutual assumption of those marital rights, duties and obligations which are usually manifested by married people, including, but not necessarily dependent on, sexual relations.

**Collusion**—An agreement by two or more persons to obtain an object forbidden by law.

**Commingle**—To combine funds or property into a common fund.

**Common-law Marriage**—One not solemnized in the ordinary way but created by an agreement to marry followed by cohabitation.

**Community Property**—Property owned in common by husband and wife each having an undivided one-half interest by reason of their marital status.

**Condonation**—Conditional forgiveness, by means of continuance or resumption of marital cohabitation, by one of the married parties, of a known matrimonial offense committed by the other that would constitute a cause of divorce.

**Complaint**—In a civil proceeding, the first pleading of the plaintiff setting out the facts on which the claim for relief is based.

**Compromise and Settlement**—An arrangement arrived at, either in court or out of court, for settling a dispute upon what appears to the parties to be equitable terms.

**Compulsory Education**—The legal obligation to attend school up to a certain age.

**Conciliation**—The adjustment and settlement of a dispute in a friendly, unantagonistic manner.

**Conclusion of Fact**—A conclusion reached by natural inference and based solely on the facts presented.

**Conclusion of Law**—A conclusion reached through the application of rules of law.

**Conclusive Evidence**—Evidence which is incontrovertible.

**Contingent**—Conditioned upon the occurrence of some future event.

**Corporal Punishment**—Physical punishment as distinguished from pecuniary punishment or a fine; any kind of punishment of, or inflicted on, the body.

**Corroborate**—To support a statement, argument, etc. with confirming facts or evidence.

**Counterclaims**—Counter-demands made by a respondent in his or her favor against a claimant.

**Court**—The branch of government responsible for the resolution of disputes arising under the laws of the government.

**Cross-Claim**—A claim litigated by co-defendants or co-plaintiffs against each other.

**Cross-Examination**—The questioning of a witness by someone other than the one who called the witness to the stand concerning matters about which the witness testified during direct examination.

**Cruel and Inhuman Treatment**—A ground for divorce. Cruel and inhuman treatment consists of cruelty, whether physical, verbal, sexual or emotional, committed by the defendant, against the plaintiff, that endangers the plaintiff's well-being and makes living together either unsafe or improper.

**De Facto**—Past act which must be accepted although illegitimate.

**Default Judgment**—A divorce judgment may be obtained against the defendant when the defendant fails to respond to the summons and or complaint for divorce within the time allowed by law.

**Defense**—Opposition to the truth or validity of the plaintiff's claims.

**Delinquent**—An infant of not more than a specified age who has violated criminal laws or has engaged in disobedient, indecent or immoral conduct, and is in need of treatment, rehabilitation, or supervision.

**Divorce**—The legal separation of a husband and wife, effected by the judgment or decree of a court.

**Discovery**—Modern pretrial procedure by which one party gains information held by another party.

**Disposition**—The process by which the juvenile court decides what is to be done with, for, or about the child who has been found to be within its jurisdiction.

**Domestic Partnership**—An ongoing relationship between two adults of the same or opposite sex who are (i) sharing a residence; (ii) over the age of 18; (iii) emotionally interdependent; and (iv) intend to reside together indefinitely.

**Domestic Relations Law**—Generally refers to the body of law that governs divorce and other matrimonial actions, also known as family or matrimonial law.

**Domicile**—The one place designated as an individual's permanent home.

**Due Process Rights**—All rights which are of such fundamental importance as to require compliance with due process standards of fairness and justice.

**Duty**—The obligation, to which the law will give recognition and effect, to conform to a particular standard of conduct toward another.

**Emancipation**—The surrender of care, custody and earnings of a child, as well as renunciation of parental duties.

**Expert Witness**—A witness who has special knowledge about a certain subject, upon which he or she will testify, which knowledge is not normally possessed by the average person.

**Eyewitness**—A person who can testify about a matter because of his or her own presence at the time of the event.

**Fact Finder**—In a judicial or administrative proceeding, the person, or group of persons, that has the responsibility of determining the acts relevant to decide a controversy.

**Fact Finding**—A process by which parties present their evidence and make their arguments to a neutral person, who issues a nonbinding report based on the findings, which usually contains a recommendation for settlement.

**Finding**—Decisions made by the court on issues of fact or law.

**Hearing**—A proceeding during which evidence is taken for the purpose of determining the facts of a dispute and reaching a decision.

**Illegitimacy**—A child who is born at a time when his parents are not married to each other.

**Illegitimate**—Illegal or improper. Also used to describe the status of children born out of wedlock.

**In Camera** Latin for "in chambers." Refers to proceedings held in the privacy of a judge's chambers.

**In Loco Parentis**—Latin for "in the place of a parent." Refers to an individual who assumes parental obligations and status without a formal, legal adoption.

**Incapacity**—Incapacity is a defense to breach of contract which refers to a lack of legal, physical or intellectual power to enter into a contract.

**Incest**—The crime of sexual intercourse or cohabitation between a man and woman who are related to each other within the degrees wherein marriage is prohibited by law.

**Infancy**—The period prior to reaching the legal age of majority.

**Infancy Presumption**—At common law, the conclusive presumption that children under the age of seven were without criminal capacity.

**Judge**—The individual who presides over a court, and whose function it is to determine controversies.

**Judgment**—A judgment is a final determination by a court of law concerning the rights of the parties to a lawsuit.

**Jurisdiction**—The power to hear and determine a case.

**Jurisprudence**—The study of legal systems and the law.

**Juvenile Court**—A court which has special jurisdiction, of a parental nature, over delinquent, dependent and neglected children.

**Kidnapping**—The illegal taking of a person against his or her will.

**Legal Aid**—A national organization established to provide legal services to those who are unable to afford private representation.

**Legal Capacity**—Referring to the legal capacity to sue, it is the requirement that a person bringing the lawsuit have a sound mind, be of lawful age, and be under no restraint or legal disability.

**Minor**—A person who has not yet reached the age of legal competence, which is designated as 18 in most states.

**Oath**—A sworn declaration of the truth under penalty of perjury.

**Objection**—The process by which it is asserted that a particular question, or piece of evidence, is improper, and it is requested that the court rule upon the objectionable matter.

**Order of Protection**—An order issued by a court that directs one individual to stop certain conduct, such as harassment, against another individual and that may order the individual to be excluded from the residence and to stay away from the other individual, his or her home, school, place of employment and his or her children.

**Overrule**—A holding in a particular case is overruled when the same court, or a higher court, in that jurisdiction, makes an opposite ruling in a subsequent case on the identical point of law ruled upon in the prior case.

**Parens Patriae**—Latin for "parent of his country." Refers to the role of the state as guardian of legally disabled individuals.

**Parties**—The disputants.

**Paternity**—The relationship of fatherhood.

**Pendente Lite**—Refers to matters that are pending until, and contingent upon, the outcome of the lawsuit.

**Petitioner**—One who presents a petition to a court or other body either in order to institute an equity proceeding or to take an appeal from a judgment.

**Plaintiff**—In a civil proceeding, the one who initially brings the lawsuit.

**Pleadings**—Refers to plaintiff's complaint which sets forth the facts of the cause of action, and defendant's answer which sets forth the responses and defenses to the allegations contained in the complaint.

**Procreation**—The generation of children.

**Rape**—The unlawful sexual intercourse with another person without his or her consent.

**Selective Emancipation**—The doctrine under which a child is deemed emancipated for only a part of the period of minority, or from only a part of the parent's rights, or for some purposes, and not for others.

**Separation Agreement**—Written arrangements concerning custody, child support, spousal support, and property division usually made by a married couple who decide to live separate and apart in contemplation of divorce.

**Service of Process**—The delivery of legal court documents, such as a complaint, to the defendant.

**Show Cause Order**—An accelerated method of starting an action, brought on by motion, which compels the opponent to respond within a shorter time period than usual.

**Single Parent Family**—A family in which one parent remains the primary caretaker of the children, and the children maintain little or no contact with the other parent.

**Status Offender**—A child who commits an act which is not criminal in nature, but which nevertheless requires some sort of intervention and disciplinary attention merely because of the age of the offender.

**Supreme Court**—In most jurisdictions, the Supreme Court is the highest appellate court, including the federal court system.

**Testify**—The offering of a statement in a judicial proceeding, under oath and subject to the penalty of perjury.

**Testimony**—The sworn statement make by a witness in a judicial proceeding.

**Trial**—The judicial procedure whereby disputes are determined based on the presentation of issues of law and fact. The trier of fact, either the judge or jury, decides issues of fact and the judge decides issues of law.

**Trial Court**—The court of original jurisdiction over a particular matter.

**Truancy**—Willful and unjustified failure to attend school by one who is required to attend.

**Unconstitutional**—Refers to a statute which conflicts with the United States Constitution rendering it void.

**Unfit**—Incompetent.

**Uniform Laws**—Laws that have been approved by the Commissioners on Uniform State Laws, and which are proposed to all state legislatures for consideration and adoption.

**Visitation**—The right of one parent to visit children of the marriage under order of the court.

**Ward**—A person over whom a guardian is appointed to manage his or her affairs.

# BIBLIOGRAPHY AND SUGGESTED READING

Alternatives to Marriage Project (Date Visited: April 2006) <http://www.unmarried.org/>.

American Bar Association Commission: Family Law Section (Date Visited: April 2006) <http://www.abanet.org/>.

American Civil Liberties Union (Date Visited: April 2006) <http://www.aclu.org/>.

Co-parent or Second-Parent Adoption by Same-Sex Parents. The American Academy of Pediatrics (AAP), February 4, 2002.

Black's Law Dictionary, Fifth Edition. St. Paul, MN: West Publishing Company, 1979.

Human Rights Campaign Foundation (Date Visited: April 2006) <http://www.hrc.org/>.

Legal Information Institute (Date Visited: April 2006) <http://www.law.cornell.edu/>.

United States Census Bureau (Date Visited: April 2006) <http://www.census.gov/>.